W9-BHX-509

Glam Italia!

H O W T O

TRAVEL ITALY

SECRETS TO GLAMOROUS TRAVEL
(ON A NOT SO GLAMOROUS BUDGET)

© 2018 Glam World Publishing LLC
All Rights Reserved.

No part of this publication may be reproduced, distributed or transmitted in any form or by any means, electronic or mechanical, including photocopying, recording, or by any information storage and retrieval system without prior written consent of Glam World Publishing LLC.

Reviewers may quote brief passages.

Email corinna@corinnabsworld.com

ISBN: 978-1-7323799-0-9 (ebook)
ISBN: 978-1-7323799-1-6 (print)

DISCLAIMER

The author is not a travel agent. All opinions and views expressed are those of the author based on personal travel experiences. Businesses, websites and apps recommended by this author may change ownership, rebrand or close, through no fault of the author. The author has not received compensation or sponsorship from any recommended businesses. (though she plans to continue visiting them!)

Cover art and all images by Marta Halama www.sonho.pl
© Glam World Publishing.

Photography by Tracy Battaglia Fully Alive Photography

Contents

INTRODUCTION

Italia ti amo

I have loved Italy for years. Decades actually.

My first trip was a lifetime ago when I was 22 years old and I took a Contiki tour around Europe, on a bus full of 18 to 35-year-olds all visiting Europe for the first time. We started in France, then travelled around Spain, back through the French Riviera and Monaco into Italy. We went to the Greek Islands, back to Italy and up through Venice, into Austria then Germany, Belgium, Holland and back to the UK. (Luxembourg and Lichtenstein were in there somewhere too.) At the time, I couldn't have planned a month-long trip around Europe to save myself, so a bus tour was perfect. It was enormous fun, I made friendships that have lasted a lifetime, had nonstop eye-opening experiences, and did many wild and wonderful things. It set the stage for a lifetime of international travel and was the beginning of my love affair with Italy.

If you are reading this book and are about to embark on a big bus tour, good for you! Hopefully you will take the information I have to share with you and use it to expand upon your Italian adventure. Bus tours can be a fun, low stress way to see many places in a short space of time. On my Contiki tour, we went to countless cities in ten different countries around Europe in only a month. Spending two or three days in a city was a great introduction to Europe. There were some cities I was glad to see but felt no need to revisit, with others I began a lifelong love affair. (I adored Salzburg but haven't returned since, Paris on the other hand became a big part of my life.)

Somewhere along the way I found myself the owner of an "accidental business" – the Glam Italia tours. I never intended to create a business taking small groups of women on private tours of Italy. It happened all by itself! Friends (then friends-of-friends, and then friends-of-friends-of-friends – there were even some strangers who tracked me down through social media!) asked me to show them the Italy they had seen in my Facebook and Instagram photos. They wanted to walk in my world for a moment – not my-single-mommy world, but the one where I was exploring and savoring Italy, doing wonderful things, meeting fun and engaging people, having the time of my life.

So, this red-haired makeup artist, from New Zealand and living in America, began designing boutique private tours for small cadres of women; women who wanted to feel a bit glamorous, see some of the big monuments, but also experience another side of Italy, the one the tour buses can't show you. And they wanted to do it on a budget. The Glam Italia Tours were born! Perhaps the popularity of the Glam Italia Tours is due to these origins. Now I take a group to Italy several times each year; this little business became the most fulfilling, rewarding, exciting métier imaginable.

I want my Glam Italia travelers to love Italy as much as I do. I want them to feel the magic that *I* feel; not to just see the big monuments and tourist attractions, but to have an experience that stays with them forever. I want them to fall in love with sitting in a beautiful piazza drinking a cappuccino and watching the world go by; to feel the magic of wandering around ancient streets in Rome – not the streets where the tour buses are parked, but where Roman residents go about their daily life. I want my travelers to sit at a local restaurant and eat a bowl of pasta that is so exquisitely delicious, they can't do anything but savor every incredible bite. And I want them to pay no more than 10 euros for that bowl of pasta!

It is important to me that my little tour groups see places the tour buses don't visit, meet Italians and discover how warm, fun-loving and friendly they are. I want them to have the time to just breathe it all in.

I invite my travelers to wander through a local village market, to experience buying a wedge of local pecorino and some bread made by local women, following the recipes their families have been using for centuries. We buy handfuls of tomatoes ripened by the Italian sun within a ten-mile radius of where we are standing, locally grown olives and a bottle of locally produced wine and enjoy a meal in an apartment we are renting that was built in the 13th century. It is an Italian experience they will never forget!

Taking group after group of travelers through "my Italy", I never tire of seeing those looks of wonder and joy on their faces. I get to watch them all fall in love with this beautiful country.

However, I came to realize that I can manage to do only a few tours per year. As a mother and busy makeup artist living in the US, taking Glam Italia tours year-round is not an option for me. I did the math and figured that at most I can show forty people per year my beloved Italy.

And so, I decided to write this book to share my way of traveling with people who want to experience some of "my Italy" and plan their own journeys. I want to help you to have the absolute trip of a lifetime, and for you to take away from this book all the inspiration and the information you need to build your own amazing Italian vacation. Hopefully my book will give you the confidence to do this, whether you're travelling alone or with a group of your friends or family.

This book will:

- help you plan your trip
- give you tips and tricks for getting amazing flight deals
- choose good, reasonably-priced places to stay
- figure out things to do
- give you help on the ground when you need it
- guide you through Italian train stations
- help you manage if you're not feeling well
- give you references to the wines and the cuisine of each region you are visiting.

By the end of your trip, you'll love Italy as much as I do!

So, let's get started…

Planning

CHAPTER ONE
How to Build Your Trip

Choose your own adventure

Where Do I Start?

One of the things I hear over and over from people who want to go to Italy is that they don't know where to begin planning a trip, which places to visit, or for how long. It's too overwhelming.

Most people start out thinking that because they are traveling all the way to Italy they need to cram in as many things as possible. That may be good advice for some countries, but I believe that Italy is a country to be savored. It is at its best when you move through it slowly, take your time and enjoy.

Whether I am planning a Glam Italia tour for a group of women, or planning a trip by myself, I always begin with the following steps:

1. WORK OUT HOW MUCH TIME YOU HAVE.

Trust me. You will never have enough time to spend in Italy and you will always leave wanting more. So, my first piece of advice is to take as many vacation days as you can. One of the groups I am taking to Italy this year wanted to go for seven or eight days. I convinced them to increase it to twelve. You'll have more fun if you're not rushing.

If you are flying across the world to get there you really need to spend as many days there as possible. If you only get a week of paid vacation, plan your trip across two weekends and take a couple of unpaid days as well. There is so much to see and do in Italy, you will be glad you took those extra days!

2. DECIDE WHAT TIME OF YEAR YOU CAN GO.

Having figured out the maximum number of vacation days you can take, you need to look at when you can go. Any time of year is a good time to go to Italy, but of course the sort of trip you have will be drastically different depending on the season.

Personally, I'd try to avoid mid-summer (unless I was staying in a villa in Puglia or somewhere along the Adriatic coast… maybe Sardinia, with nothing to do but swimming and relaxing). **The weather in July and August is incredibly hot.** Too hot for some people (me!) to enjoy walking around sightseeing. I do know plenty of people who travel to Italy in July and love it, and if July was the only month I was able to travel I would still go, but I would definitely build my trip around the heat (see my earlier comment about a villa in Puglia!).

Another important factor to consider is that **July is peak tourist season** in Italy. In July, everything costs more, there can be longer wait times to get into tourist attractions, the coast roads are busier, and most of the beaches are packed with people. The big tourist cities (like Rome and Florence) are more crowded. Some people love the tourist buzz, but others find it more enjoyable to visit cities and regions that are less popular with tourists during this time.

The further south you travel, the hotter it gets. If you don't do well in the heat, July can be a wonderful month to travel through the mountain regions and the north of Italy, where the air is cooler. If you crave sunshine and blue skies and have dreamed about beaches in Italy, you will love traveling in July.

August is the month that Europeans take their summer vacations. The beach areas are *packed* and traffic along the coasts is very heavy because everyone brings their cars. The 45-minute drive from Salerno to Positano on the Amalfi Coast can take more than three hours in August! And it is so very, very hot. Every beach area and every lake area you can think of will be full, and the cities will be scorched.

In the US, we have endless air conditioning everywhere, so if it's hot out we can stay indoors, or at the end of a long day at the beach we can come inside and chill out in the cool air. In Italy, much of the accommodation either doesn't have any air conditioning, or doesn't have particularly effective air conditioning, so you often just can't escape the heat.

On the other hand, if I could stay in the giant apartment in an old palace I once rented in Puglia, right on the water, with huge Moroccan windows that caught the ocean breeze, and if I didn't have to go anywhere or do anything apart from swim in the Adriatic and eat the local cuisine, I would be blissful there for the entire two months!

My favorite times to travel to Italy are in June and September, when the weather is gorgeous but not too hot, you can swim but you can also be comfortable just wandering around checking out all the sights.

Easter is a huge event in Italy. **April** can be glorious, especially if you want to do lots of walking. **May** can be rainy, or it can be perfect. **October** is when the olive harvest happens, and you can get wonderful weather. I love going in **December** and wandering through the Christmas markets, enjoying a relatively tourist-free experience. Every month has something to offer, you just have to plan your expectations around the weather.

Many of the restaurants and shops in the touristy coastal areas close over the winter months, so you need to do a little research and factor that in to your equation as well.

If you have a set time of year when you can take your vacation, build your itinerary around what the weather is likely to be like, which may mean changing some of the things you want to do. If I were going in March (Spring), I wouldn't be planning on sailing around Capri, or lying in the sun and swimming in the blue Tyrrhenian Sea. Instead I would plan endless long days of walking around Pompeii and Herculaneum and exploring Naples and Caserta.

If you have flexibility in when you can travel, then build your trip based on the things you would like to experience.

3. MAKE A LIST OF WHAT YOU WANT TO SEE AND DO.

When I am building a Glam Italia tour, I make sure I understand exactly what each particular group is interested in. Do they want to see art and churches and architecture, or are they more about shopping and beaches? Maybe they want a little of both? Do they get carsick or seasick? Are they able to do a lot of walking? Can they tackle multiple flights of stairs? Many apartments in Italy are up several flights of stairs and rarely have elevators.

To help me figure this out, I give my travelers a questionnaire and ask them to list fifty things they want to see and do in Italy. (You can get the PDF of this at: www.glamitaliabooks.com/freeresources)

In the questionnaire, I suggest a few things like the Colosseum, the Vatican, Michelangelo's David, the gondolas in Venice and the Duomo in Florence, just to get them started. Some people print off multiple pages and fill in endless lists of things they are interested in seeing and doing; others struggle to fill one page. I direct them towards my Pinterest boards (@Corinnamakeup) which are full of Italy stories, with lots of pins about different areas in Italy. I also suggest that they start researching things to do in Italy on Pinterest. There is a wealth of information there, (with pictures!) that can help you to flesh out your list. There will be plenty of places to visit and things to do that you will have never heard of before but would find fascinating.

Definitely look beyond the main cities and the main tourist spots. If you are thinking about staying in Florence, google "Day trips from Florence". If planning on staying in Rome, search "Unusual things to do in Rome". I suggest googling things to do *around* the areas where you will be staying. For a Glam Italia tour, I always have a full schedule planned, but Italy is so saturated with amazing historical sites, ancient little villages, incredible ruins, church art in tiny out of the way villages and towns, and generally fascinating things to see, it would be a shame to return home and find you had been just a couple of miles away from something you would have loved to have seen or done. For example, if you are in Florence, you may want to take a day trip to the market in Arezzo or to the castle in Poppi. Perhaps you would enjoy shopping at the giant Prada outlet in Montevarchi. From Rome, a day trip to Tivoli to see Villa d'Este and Hadrian's Villa is spectacular, or maybe you would enjoy a quick train ride to wander the streets of Viterbo or Orvieto?

Don't be intimidated about getting from one place to another. Italy is easy to get around. If you really want to explore a region, you can rent a car and drive around, or hire a driver, but generally the train system is fantastic and will carry you all over the country quickly and inexpensively. If you want to do a day trip to another town, it's easy to just jump on a train. For example, if you are based in Rome but want to see Venice, you can buzz up there for the day on the fast train – it only takes about 3 ½ hours each way. If you are based in Florence but have always wanted to see Capri, no problem! Take the fast train to Naples, then a ferry or hydrofoil over to Capri. The last boat departs Capri around 6:30pm, so you can be back in Florence by about 10:30pm. Most cities and towns are really accessible, and when you see how easy it is to move around, the entire country and all of its possibilities open up to you.

Once you have your list of what you want to see, do, you can start building your trip.

4. MAKE A LIST OF EXPERIENCES YOU WOULD LIKE TO HAVE.

This is the most important thing to consider as you plan your trip. I don't know anyone who has said, "I want to trudge around in the heat with a group of 40 other people, following a guide waving an umbrella, listening to her drone on about what I'm walking past, via a headset that crackles in and out."

Italy is so much more than just a list of monuments. It is a country to *experience*. If you race around the big tourist sights, getting the postcard photos that you've seen a hundred times over (albeit now with the heads of other tourists in your shot) then you are missing the magic of Italy.

So, start making a list of *experiences* you would like to have. Let your imagination go. You might start with sitting at a table in a beautiful old piazza with a cappuccino and a slice of panforte, just watching the world go by.

Or maybe you imagine yourself sitting on a terrace in the late afternoon, with a breathtaking view over the rolling hills and vineyards of Tuscany, a glass of red wine in your hand and a leather-bound journal on the table in front of you, waiting for you to record your day's adventures.

Perhaps you would like to experience discovering some little town well off the beaten path, far from the tourist crush, and wandering its streets until you find a darling little restaurant with only five tables, stopping there and having the best meal of your life.

You may be thinking about breaking out your most gorgeous swimsuit and stretching out on a sun chair under a blue and white striped umbrella at a lido somewhere on the Italian Riviera, soaking up the Mediterranean sun, before diving into the ocean.

Maybe you want to ride around on the back of a Vespa driven by a handsome Italian fellow with glossy black hair and olive skin.

Maybe you want to sit quietly, by yourself, soaking up the majesty of Botticelli's Venus, Cimabue's Crucifixion or Sanmartino's Veiled Christ.

Maybe you want to attend mass at St Peter's Basilica in Vatican City, or in a teeny tiny church on top of a hill in Umbria.

Imagine walking around the local market with a chef, choosing fresh produce, then going back to a beautiful villa for an Italian cooking lesson; then spending all morning cooking, and all afternoon on the back terrace with a gorgeous view, eating the meal you prepared, drinking local wine and talking for hours…

If you have read Marlena de Blasi's book, *A Thousand Days in Venice*, maybe you too would love to experience sitting in a coffee bar far from the Grand Canal tourist crush and meeting the man of your dreams who has fallen in love with your profile across the piazza. (It really did happen!)

Perhaps you imagine yourself driving up the winding road to Cortona and wandering through the streets you know so well from reading Frances Mayes' books.

This is where the magic really happens. Think about the experiences you would like to have, and build your trip around them.

A lady on one of my Glam Italia tours dreamed of riding a bicycle through fields of sunflowers. She even brought the dress she had pictured herself wearing on the bike. I couldn't find her a bike to borrow, but I did get her to fields of sunflowers and took about a thousand photos of her swanning around in her dress under a crazy blue Tuscan sky. For her, it was one of the defining moments of her trip and she will never ever forget the experience.

Another of my Glam Italia women dreamed of swimming in Capri. We went by boat to a private cove where she jumped off 2000-year-old Roman ruins into the bluest water she had ever seen. (The rest of us were more intimidated by heights and just dove off the boat to swim!)

I keep my Glam Italia groups really small, with only 3–6 travelers per tour, which means we can chase the wonderful individual experiences and do the super special things.

When I think back over all my trips to Italy, the highlights are the incredible experiences I've had, much more so than the monuments I've photographed. To me, Rome isn't about the Vatican or the Colosseum, although I do love both. Rome is wandering along the little cobblestoned streets of the Trastevere, sitting on a wall up on the Janiculum while watching the sun set over this beautiful city, drinking wine and eating artichokes al fresco in the Jewish Ghetto, and watching Italian movies on a hot summer night, at the outdoor screen in the piazza two blocks from my apartment.

As time goes by you won't remember all the names of all the things you see, but you *will* remember your experiences and how those experiences made you feel.

Making a list of experiences you want to have, and building your trip around that list, will define your Italian adventure and transform it into the trip of a lifetime.

5. COLOR OUTSIDE THE LINES.

Most people, when making their first trip to Italy, only look at the most famous places – Venice, Florence, Rome, the Amalfi Coast, maybe Cinqueterre, Pisa and Tuscany. Each and every one of these options *is* completely fantastic. I have visited each many, many times and will continue to go back many, many more, but Italy is so much more than these places!

There are many fantastic spots all over Italy that will totally wow you, and you're likely to get a better view of them than somewhere you're fighting crowds of tourists. Exploring these areas will often end up being the highlight of your trip.

Puglia

One of my favorite regions in Italy is Puglia. Puglia is gorgeous, easy to drive around, incredibly affordable, full of fascinating history, and has vastly fewer tourists than the rest of Italy. It looks quite different from the rest of the country too, with little white-washed towns overlooking the sensationally blue Adriatic and Ionian seas, the trulli houses, the low plains with their endless vineyards and fields of ancient olive trees.

Puglia is slightly flatter than the rest of the country – it's as if the mountains came racing down from the north and ran out of steam once they found the heel of Italy's boot. I personally know perhaps only ten people who have been to Puglia, and of that ten, three came with me on a tour, and the fourth is my mother!

One of the most beautiful cities you could ever visit is Lecce, "the Florence of the south", deep down in Puglia. If you take the time to go to Lecce you will fall in love with the architecture, the piazzas and the pretty streets. You will also see a fraction of the tourists you find in Florence.

Basilicata

Basilicata is the driest (and at one point was the poorest) region in Italy. It makes up the arch of the boot of Italy, sharing borders with Puglia, Calabria and Campania. Basilicata has two coastlines, a shorter coastline on the Tyrrhenian Sea between Calabria and Campania and a longer coastline between Puglia and Calabria along the Gulf of Taranto.

When you cross from Puglia to Basilicata the landscape changes again, as does the architecture. A trip to Matera, a city in Basilicata that has been continuously inhabited since the Paleolithic age, will change you forever. You will recognize the Sassi, an area of Matera that is full of cave dwellings, from movies such as *The Passion of the Christ*. It looks different, not only from everywhere else you might visit in Italy, but from almost anywhere else in the world.

Sicily

Sicily is absolutely magnificent. It remains largely off the main tourist radars, which makes it even more fabulous. Every time I go to Sicily I dream about coming back and staying for at least a month, there is so much to see and do here! Throughout history, largely defenseless Sicily has been conquered and run by one country after another. From the Greeks to the Romans, the Germans to the Byzantine, to the Vikings, the Normans, the Spanish and the Bourbons, each leaving behind their own influence on the architecture, culture and cuisine, making Sicily one of the most layered and textured places I have ever visited. On top of this, it is devastatingly beautiful, and the people are incredibly warm and friendly – it is hard not to fall in love with Sicily!

Maybe instead of going to Tuscany look at **Umbria**, **Abruzzo**, **Le Marche** or **Emilio Romagna**. Each of these regions is different from the next and has its own amazing sights to visit. They all have their own wines, their own specialized cuisine, their own stories and their own culture.

The point I'm trying to make is that you can get almost everywhere in Italy quite easily and there is so much to see! I have come to realize that if I live to be 100 and were to spend every single day from now until then exploring Italy, I still wouldn't see it all.

Italy is full of amazing places to see and things to do. You can make your trip richer by splitting your time between the more famous cities and some of the other places that don't have so many tourists. When I'm building a trip, I try to include a mixture of big tourist areas and places completely off the beaten path.

Find Your Favorites

My absolute favorite places are the little towns I stumble upon that don't have any t-shirt shops, where tour buses don't stop, and that get very little tourism. Have a look on Pinterest, do some google searches, read some travel blogs, find out about some of these fabulous towns and villages and add some into your itinerary, even if only for a day trip. My Italian home is the medieval hilltop Tuscan town of San Gimignano. Some of my best discoveries have been from driving around the area with no particular destination in mind. I found Certaldo Alto with its 12th century palace, Colle Val d'Elsa, another medieval town with a moat and a pretend castle (they couldn't afford the real thing and wanted invaders to think twice before attacking), and the artsy little two-street town of Casole d'Elsa. I always take my tour groups to Volterra, a magnificent hilltop town well off the beaten path, that is spectacular in its own right but also contains the ruins of a 1st century Roman amphitheater.

6. IT'S OKAY TO SEPARATE FROM THE GROUP.

Remember our goal is to build the trip of a lifetime for *you*. Just because you are traveling with family, friends, or a group doesn't mean you can't step away for a day (or every day) to go look at things that you personally find interesting. You need to make sure that this trip is completely fantastic for *you*, and that you are not just dragging yourself along behind the people you are with, doing only what *they* want to do.

For example, if I were taking a trip to Florence with friends, I would hate it if all we were doing was looking at shops. I'd want to look at art and architecture and wander around, exploring the city. My friends might just want to take advantage of the designer outlets, the handmade shoes and the leather jackets. In that scenario, no one is wrong – everyone should be able to maximize their own experience. I'm also not a believer in travel compromise. You each have a limited amount of time to see and do everything that interests you. Who knows if or when you might get back?

Italy is incredibly safe and easy to move around, so if you want to do something different from your travel companions, go do it! Meet up later for lunch or dinner and tell each other what you have seen and done. That way everyone is happy and contented.

7. PLOT IT ON A MAP.

Once you have a nice long list of things you would like to see and do, sit down with a map and see where everything is in relation to each other. You will never get to everything on your list (if you do, your list wasn't big enough!). There will be things that just aren't feasible for this particular trip, usually due to weather, the time of year you are traveling, or the distance you would have to travel to get to them. But, by plotting your plans on a map, you will be able to see which things could fit together or are easily accessible to one another.

For Example...

For example, say your list included: Venice, Verona, Cinqueterre, Florence, wine-tasting in the Chianti, Pisa, Cortona and Orvieto. You could do all of those things as day trips from a central base in

Florence. You could rent a car or hire a driver to take you wine tasting and to Cortona, but travel to everywhere else by train. If Rome, Naples, the Amalfi Coast, Capri and Paestum were also on your list, you could stay somewhere on the Amalfi Coast for a few days and buzz back up to Rome for the final days of your trip.

If you had twelve days to spend in Italy, and had all of those on your list, plus Matera, then you would have to choose something to miss this time around. Matera is a little trickier and more time consuming to get to, so maybe you would take it off the list for this trip, or maybe you would skip your days in Verona and Cinqueterre, or Pisa and Orvieto. Or if you hired a driver you could visit Pisa, then the Chianti, and then Cortona in one day visit, killing three birds with one stone.

The key is to see where everything is on the map, see which things you can group together, and plan your trip that way.

8. CHOOSE YOUR HOME BASES.

So much time is wasted on trips when you keep moving from one location to the next. The time spent re-packing, checking out of your accommodation, moving to the next spot, waiting to check in to your next accommodation, and checking in all adds up and takes away from your vacation time. It can also be completely and utterly exhausting!

I like to stay in two or three places and do day trips from each one.

Once you have refined the list of places you want to visit, and plotted it out on the map, then it's time to decide in which two or three places you want to stay. From there you can decide whether you want to stay in the city, or maybe in a nearby village in the countryside. I love Florence and stay there from time to time, but normally if I am in the area I will stay in San Gimignano. That means renting a car and driving around Tuscany, which I love to do. However, if I am traveling on a budget, I will stay in Florence and save the cost of the rental car.

9. RESEARCH LOCAL EVENTS.

Every city, town and village in Italy has its own annual festival as well as a variety of other festivals throughout the year. Some of them are celebrations of the story of that particular town, with the townsfolk all dressing up in period costume and acting out their history. Others are religious festivals celebrating the patron saint of the town, or a celebration of the Virgin Mary, or some point in religious history.

Some towns have food festivals or wine festivals or olive festivals or music festivals. Wooden tables are set up, everyone comes and there is eating and dancing and socializing. They are *so much fun*! Whatever the festival, you do not want to miss it!

I always do a little extra research and move my trips around to make sure I don't miss whatever is happening. If I am taking a Glam Italia group somewhere nearby I arrange our plans so that we can attend any local festivals.

In **Sicily** we were able to watch the entire town of Giardini Naxos get dressed in costume and parade along the beachfront promenade, with huge floats and singing and candles, culminating in a fabulous fireworks display over the ocean.

In **Salerno** I took a group to the San Matteo festival, and while visiting at Christmas one year I saw a big religious parade in the historical center of town. Every summer I try to co-ordinate being in **San Gimignano**, either with a tour group or with friends and family, for the Ferie delle Messi, the town's medieval festival. These festivals involve the whole town, and locals come from nearby towns to take part in the festivities. Everyone is in medieval costume, there are games and flag dances and food stalls and music. They are not only exciting to witness and be a part of, but they also help you to understand the history of the town and the deep connection the people whose families have lived here for centuries feel for it.

On another vacation we were in **Rapallo**, on the Italian Riviera, for their Green Carpet event. A green carpet was rolled out along the entire length of the ocean promenade and every restaurant had tables set up on it, with specialty menus created just for that night. Every bar made a special drink. The entire town came out for the event. It was incredibly good fun and one of those fantastic travel experiences that we still talk about years later.

In **Ravello** on the Amalfi Coast, we sat out under the stars at Villa Rufalo for an evening at their summer music festival.

In **Florence** we have been to the historical football matches (Calcio Historico) in Piazza Santa Croce.

After years and years of vacations in Italy, I have been so lucky to go to many, many festivals. It is a fantastic slice of Italian life to witness, participate in, and make a part of your vacation. When we travel we don't just go to see monuments and churches and beautiful views, we also travel to experience the world, learn the history and the customs of the places we visit. I advise you to grab every opportunity to participate in a local festival or event during your time in Italy. It will completely enrich your journey.

10. READ BOOKS AND WATCH MOVIES SET IN ITALY.

I love reading books written by people who have moved to Italy. Especially books by people who have bought centuries-old homes in Italy and refurbished them. I can read these endlessly, perhaps because it fits into some secret dream I have of doing the same. I also love movies set in Italy. Apart from the magic of disappearing into a fantasy Italian life for a couple of hours, books and movies serve as particularly fabulous research.

Movies give you magnificent visuals that may inspire you to seek out certain experiences. There's nothing like watching someone blissfully cycle down a Tuscan country lane to make you want to do the same. Countless people have made the trek to Cortona after watching Frances Mayes'/Diane Lane's *Under the Tuscan Sun*. Many viewers decided they had to experience Elizabeth Gilbert's/Julia Roberts' Rome after watching *Eat Pray Love*. Movies are a great source of inspiration for places and experiences you may want to add to your trip. And both of those movies were based on books!

Where movies can provide an inspiring visual fantasy, books can be an amazing resource for details. I get so much specific information from books. I have been to most of the restaurants that **Frances Mayes** talks about in her books on Tuscany. I found my way to the Aeolian Islands after reading about them in **Laura Fraser**'s autobiography, *An Italian Affair*. I went to Casa Cuseni after reading **Daphne Phelps** book, *A House in Sicily*, set in Taormina. (I even managed to get a private viewing of the Picasso in the office there!) **John Berendt** and **Barry Frangipane** have shown me a whole new Venice via their books, changing how I spend every moment in that beautiful city.

I read every book I can get my hands on that involves someone moving to Italy, and I make lists of wonderful places to visit that I have discovered by reading about them in books. (You'll find a list of **15 Books Set in Italy You Need to Know About** on my *Corinna B's World* blog.) https://corinnabsworld.com/2018/05/15-books-set-in-italy-that-you-need-to-know-about.html

One of my favorite books was written by **Michael Rips**, a lawyer from Nebraska who with his wife moved to a tiny little town, 50 kilometers from Rome, so that she could devote a year to painting. Every day he would sit at a café in the piazza with his laptop, working on his book and observing all the fantastic characters who lived there.

It took me a while to find the town in the book because it doesn't show up on most maps. Then it took months to find a place to stay because almost no tourists go there and there are very few hotels. In the end, I rented a thousand-year-old tower that had been converted into an apartment and I made the pilgrimage. It was well worth the effort! Due to the scarcity of travelers through this town, everyone knew us when we arrived and they all wanted to chat. My Italian wasn't very strong at the time so my telling them that I had *read* Michael's book was initially interpreted as my being Michael's *friend who was learning Italian*. Regardless, the townsfolk undertook to help me learn the language. Every time I stopped for coffee or for a glass of wine, every time I parked my car or walked up the hill from the ruins, someone would come and greet me. They would tell me stories about their town, draw me maps of cool things to go see, and delightfully, tolerate my butchering their beautiful language while patiently helping me to get it right.

Never in a million years would I have stumbled upon this lovely place had I not read about it in Michael's book. (I never tell anyone the name of the town because I have a terrible fear that I will go back and find tour buses parked along the hillside.) You'll just have to read the book yourself.

11. RESEARCH YOUR TRANSPORT OPTIONS.

When you have a rough idea of the areas you want to visit you can refine it further by looking at your transport options. These days, figuring out how to get around Italy is as easy as asking Google how to get from place A to place B.

Rental Car

A rental car opens up another world of choices to you when traveling in Italy. You couldn't pay me to drive inside Rome, Naples, Palermo, or even Florence, but over the years I have driven extensively all over Italy and Sicily. In fact, before I discovered the train system I would just drive everywhere!

Some of my best Italian vacations ever were with one of my best friends. We would rent an apartment in an ancient palazzo in San Gimignano and each day we would point the old Fiat Panda in a different direction and explore. Every little town had (and still has) its own market day, so we would ask which town had its market that day, and go buy fresh cheese and prosciutto, salad items, bread and olives, and then drive back to our apartment and have the best meal ever. We discovered many towns and villages that weren't in the guide books and that to this day are among my favorites in all of Italy.

We got lost over and over again, which I loved, because getting lost in Italy means you are about to discover some fabulous new place. We spoke no Italian and there weren't translation apps for our phones back then, but we usually managed to communicate to the locals that we were lost. More than once, someone got in their car and led us back to the motorway (or to wherever we were trying to go).

Racing through the hills of the Chianti in our Fiat Panda, playing Italian pop music on the radio, we found old abandoned houses to explore. I took hundreds of photos of them, sure that one day I would come back and buy one. (Who knows – maybe I still will!) Some were magnificent, centuries old with huge wood-burning ovens in the backyard, broken-down and overgrown vineyards on the property, and their own 600-year-old church all boarded up. These vacations were 80% about the experience and 20% about looking at famous sites. They were magnificent.

However, if driving an Italian road is something that you would find stressful, don't do it. It's easily avoided. There's no need to have you frazzled behind the wheel of a car when you should be enjoying your incredible Italian vacation.

Train

If this is your first trip to Italy, or if the thought of driving in a foreign country is overwhelming, you can easily plan your trip by train. The Italian train system is fantastic. There are little local trains that you can use to get around within each region and there are high-speed trains to take you from one big city to another, or to get you from one end of the country to the other.

The high-speed trains are my favorite way to travel across the country. You sit in big, comfortable seats, there is a buffet car if you are hungry, a drink service (depending on which class you book), and best of all you feel like you are living inside a National Geographic episode, watching through huge picture windows as Italy passes by. I have flown into Milan and then taken the high-speed train all the way to Salerno on several occasions just because the view is so spectacular!

The train system opens up the entire country to you. You can get everywhere, easily, safely and inexpensively.

Car/Train Combo

Even if you are comfortable driving you may want to split your travel between rental cars and trains.

For example, if you were staying in Lucca with a rental car, but wanted to go to Venice for the day, rather than drive you'd be wiser to leave the car behind and take the intercity train to Florence and then the high-speed train to Venice. This would take less time, be less expensive and be much more relaxing than driving.

Bus

There are also good bus options available. This past summer I needed to get a group from the Italian Riviera to Florence. The train would have meant hauling suitcases up and down several flights of stairs and using several train stations, each with more stairs and no elevators. A private driver would have been too expensive from Santa Margherita Ligure to Florence. However, it was not expensive from Santa Margherita to Genoa, so we had a driver take us to the bus station in Genoa and took a Flix bus to Florence.

The bus was modern and super comfortable, the bus driver had our names on his list and was waiting outside the bus to check us in and to load our luggage. It was my first time using the bus service, and it was brilliant as well as ridiculously cheap. It was only around 20 euros per ticket!

You may find that some of the places on your list may be too tricky or time consuming to get to, but most places are incredibly easy.

Hire a Driver

Hiring a driver is another great option. It allows you to get out and explore without the stress of reading maps and figuring out toll booths and motorways. If you decide to hire a driver, book as quickly as possible, because they are usually heavily booked.

I used to do all the driving on the Amalfi Coast for my tours but that meant I couldn't have a glass of wine at lunch (and just between you and me, the drive up the hill to Ravello was nerve-racking), so I started hiring a driver. I have an amazing company that I use for all my Naples and Amalfi Coast runs, and they are the first people I book when setting up a new tour. Most of these companies are small, owner-operated businesses. I suggest you look on TripAdvisor for companies working on the Amalfi Coast and read their reviews. Any company with consistently good reviews will be good to go with. (If you would like a list of my personal drivers and tour guides, etc, you can sign up to my mailing list at HowToTravelItaly.net)

I do suggest you consider all the different travel options, how they fit in with your itinerary, your budget and your comfort zone.

Planning Travel with Children

Traveling with children can be a blessing or a curse. Days spent at the Colosseum in the heat can be a nightmare for little ones; days at the beach can be amazing. You know your children and what they can handle.

My son has traveled the world with me since he was a baby. Luckily for me he loves to travel. One thing I have always done is give him a list in advance of every place we're going and task him with finding at **least one thing of interest** *to him* for us to see or do in each place. When he was little I helped him research things, but by the time he could work a computer he wanted to do it all himself.

This turned out to be a fantastic way to travel! Everywhere we went we saw so many things that were fascinating to both of us. Seeing Italy through his eyes was wonderful. He found so many quirky, weird and fun things to put on his list that were fascinating to a little boy, and we would then seek them out to visit. I loved it because these were things I would never have known about, so they were new to me too, and the joy on his face was priceless. The exercise always made him feel like an important part of our trip because he was involved in the planning. It's worth trying this approach with your kids if you are going to be traveling with them.

One more tip: **crouch down to their height and look at what they see.** You might be looking at some incredible Roman amphitheater but maybe all they can see is the backs of adults' legs. It can be frightening, claustrophobic and overwhelming to them, whether they are little kids or young tweens. Sometimes just being aware of that can motivate you to move away from the crowd and maneuver into a space where they can see everything and not feel so overwhelmed.

29

If you're travelling with children, it is a good idea to balance your trip so there is as much sightseeing as there is time for them to be free and run around.

One of my favorite trips with my son was when he was 12 years old. We were in Italy for several weeks and spent the last week on the Italian Riviera staying in a town called **Rapallo**. We wanted to spend our first day at the beach, so went to a lovely lido we found while walking down the beachfront. It was an introduction to lido-life. Families come from Milan for an entire month and book a group of beach chairs and sun umbrellas as well as a mini cabana to store their towels and beach toys and beach gear. When we arrived on the first day the people running the lido chose sun chairs and an umbrella for us that were in the middle of a bunch of families with boys.

We had been sitting down for about five minutes when a mother walked up to us with her boys in tow and asked my son's name, then she said, "Come on, Tommy, we want you to play with us." From that moment, my son had nonstop children to play with and he had the time of his life! Even though he didn't speak Italian and the other boys didn't speak English, they all spoke the language of summer fun. They took paddle boats out, swam, jumped off giant inflatables moored offshore, ran around and had an amazing time. We changed our original plans and instead went to the lido each day. He made so many new friends, and so did I!

In the evenings we would go walking after dinner, as most families do there, instead of lying around watching TV. My boy would find his new friends and they would spend the evening running around kicking a soccer ball and having fun. To this day that was one of our favorite vacations ever.

CHAPTER TWO
How Long Should You
Stay in Each Place?

There's never enough time

Once you've decided which cities, towns and villages you want to visit, and you know how many days you can spend on the ground in Italy, you need to decide where you will be overnighting and for how many nights in each place. (Remember, my first goal is to get you to travel Italy, and my second goal is to get you to explore some of the areas that have fewer tourists.)

Here's How to Figure it Out

I am going to use Venice, Florence, the broader Tuscany, Rome and Amalfi Coast as examples, because most prospective travelers are familiar with them.

I recommend that you choose two or three locations to stay in if you are planning on moving around the country. Ideally the fewer, the better. Don't waste your hard-earned holiday time on packing, repacking, checking-out of one place and waiting to check-in to the next. Vacation time is short enough as it is.

Consider the list you made of the things you want to see, and the list of the experiences you want to have. (I always let the Experiences List take precedence over the Things to See and Do List.) From there, you can figure out how long you'll need to stay in each place.

FOR EXAMPLE… TUSCANY, FLORENCE, VENICE

If your lists involve exploring villages, taking wine tours, having a cooking lesson, going to local farmers' markets, seeing Etruscan ruins or old Roman amphitheaters and spending time wandering and exploring back roads and little towns, and you are doing a mix of cities plus the Tuscan countryside, you may want to devote more days to staying in Tuscany, choosing a Tuscan town as a base for the first half of your trip, and from there make day trips to Venice and Florence.

If your list is populated with 101 things to do in Florence, but you would like to go to the Prada outlet in Montevarchi, see the Arezzo market and visit Cortona to live out your *Under the Tuscan Sun* dream, then you would be better to base yourself in Florence for several days, hire a driver (or rent a car) for a day and do Monteverchi, Arezzo and Cortona all in one day.

If your Venice list has the Doges' Palace, St Mark's Square, Ca' D'Oro and maybe wander a little, you could do a day trip to Venice from your Florentine base. However, if your Venice list also includes trips to Burano to see the lace-making and Murano to see the glass-blowing, you want to go to Lido and Torcello, you want to photograph the Basilica Santa Maria Della Salute in the blue hour*, plus lots of idle wandering and exploring, breathing in the magic that is Venice, then that's going to take longer, and you'll need to plan a few days there.

Whereas, if you want to see Florence but it isn't a major item on your list, then I would recommend staying in Venice for several days and doing a day trip to Florence.

When you are planning the activities you want to do in the bigger cities, make sure you factor in time spent waiting in line, the time inside the venue, and the commute in between. It is a good idea to pre-book tickets to major museums and monuments online. It doesn't mean you will just walk right in, but the pre-booked ticket lines do move more quickly.

The Blue Hour*

For those of you not familiar with the blue hour, it is this magic time at twilight, where the sun is at just the right depth below the horizon to take on a blue shade. On cloudless days the color can be really intense. There are other places around the world where the blue hour is spectacular to see and to photograph, but with Venice already being so visually unique and with the added benefit of all the water that makes up the lagoon and the canals, the blue hour in Venice is mesmerizing. For any photographer, amateur photographer or budding photographer this thirty-minute window could be the defining moment of your entire Italian adventure.

The last high-speed train out of Venice at night leaves around 7–7:30pm, so unless you are there in the winter months the blue hour needs at least one overnight stay. However, before you give away that dream of photographing the blue hour because it doesn't fit in with your travel companions' plans, or because you don't have an overnight in Venice on the itinerary, stop and ask yourself when you are likely to be back in Venice again to take up that opportunity? How much does it mean to you? You could separate from the group for one night and throw a change of clothes into a backpack. While they head back to home-base for the night, you catch the blue hour and a hotel in Venice! Anything is possible.

Beware Over-scheduling

On a map of Rome, the Colosseum, Trevi Fountain, Spanish Steps and Vatican are all quite close to one another, so you may think you can do it all in a day… but it would be a hellish day. Firstly, they are all high tourist areas, which means long wait times and large crowds of people during the busy tourist season. When you include the time spent waiting in line (even with a tour group or pre-purchased tickets), the Vatican museums, Sistine Chapel and St Peter's on a guided tour takes between three and four hours, a tour of the Colosseum, Palatine Hill and Forum needs around three hours. If you add the walk to the Trevi Fountain and the Spanish Steps and the crowds you will see at both, you will have given yourself a very overwhelming and stressful day!

I would recommend visiting the Colosseum and the Vatican on different days and leaving the afternoon and evening of each day free to wander around and see some of the other amazing sights in Rome. Across two days, I suggest you have lazy lunches in the Monti and the Trastevere, and then have a dinner in the Jewish Ghetto and another in Trastevere (my favorite neighborhood in Rome).

People tell me that they really need only one day in Rome. This sucks the wind right out of me! Before you dismiss Rome with just a day or two, know that Rome is one of the most incredible cities in the world, with so much to see and do, one lifetime is not enough to experience it all. (I once tried to make a list of my top twenty things to do in Rome and couldn't get my list below a hundred.)

FOR EXAMPLE… ROME & THE AMALFI COAST

Using our examples of Venice, Florence and Tuscany, and breaking up the first part of the trip as we did above, I would then go back to your list of things to see and do, and your list of the experiences you want to have and look at how to break up Rome and the Amalfi Coast.

The fast train from Rome to Naples, the gateway to the Amalfi Coast, takes an hour and ten minutes, which is probably less time than plenty of you spend on your commute home from work each day.

If your list has a day trip to Capri and you also want to explore Pompeii and Herculaneum then you might consider basing yourself in Rome and just taking the train back and forth, making these into two separate day trips. Pompeii and Herculaneum are both suburbs of Naples and can be seen in one day. The ferry to Capri is a 10-minute cab ride from the Naples train station, making a day on the island an easily achievable day trip from Rome.

If your list has lots of things to see and do in the Amalfi Coast area, such as visiting Pompeii and Capri but you also want to have lunch in Ravello, swim in Positano, drink limoncello in Sorrento, see the veiled Christ and the underground city in Naples, then I would suggest building your trip around several days on the Amalfi Coast and then moving to Rome for your last couple of days (especially if you are flying out of Rome).

As you can see, the more time and effort you put into your two lists, the easier it is to calculate how many days you need to stay in each area.

Experiences vs Sights

When I first took my Glam Italia tours on day trips to Capri I would have a list of 20 sights in the area, of which we would see eight or nine. Then one day I decided to change it up. I offered them the choice of spending a day seeing all those wonderful sights, or instead spending a few hours floating around the island on a boat, swimming in private coves in the Tyrrhenian Sea, having a late lunch on the patio of my favorite restaurant there and catching two of the sights on the other list before heading back to Sorrento, where we were based. Without fail, everyone wanted the experience of glamorously circumnavigating the island on a chartered boat, diving into the ocean and swimming with the view of the Fraglioni, lying under the sun to dry off on the deck. On each tour, this was consistently one of their favorite days. They could not believe they were able to have that once-in-a-lifetime experience.

On my most recent tour while we were swimming off the coast of Capri in the bluest water you have ever seen, talking about life and men and shopping and food, with a view of the Fraglioni and our boat captain singing to us a few meters away, one of my travelers got quite teary eyed because she just could not believe that she was living inside this moment, and that this was her life! She probably couldn't tell you where we ate or what else we saw in Capri, but she will always remember the *experience* of her day on the boat.

My Three Rules

When you are planning where to stay and how many days to have in each place these are my three rules:

- Stay in fewer locations.
- Experiences first. Build your itinerary around the experiences you want to have rather than how many things you want to see.

- Go slowly. Italy is best savored at a slower pace. The worst thing that you can do is to try and squeeze too many things into one day.

Or Simplify

Consider staying in just one place. I have to move around the country all the time when I am accompanying my tours, but when I go by myself I like to stay in just one place. Everywhere you go in Italy there is so much to see; you will never, ever run out of things to do.

When I am on a tight budget, I stay in a city that has good train access so that I don't have to rent a car. When I have a little more money, I hire a car and stay in a village or town far from the cities; I spend my days driving around exploring the countryside and discovering more little towns and villages.

The more time you spend just wandering and exploring, the more Italy will embrace your soul.

CHAPTER THREE
How to Choose Accommodation
& Which Neighborhood to Stay In

So many glamorous choices!

You've decided on the towns and cities you want to overnight in; now you have to decide what type of accommodation you want, and which neighborhood to stay in.

First let's consider the types of accommodation on offer.

There are of course hotels, and within the hotel selection there will be everything from large hotels to small boutique hotels to choose from. (A hotel is an *albergo*; a boutique, smaller hotel is an *albergetto*.) Then there are Bed and Breakfasts, rented rooms, vacation rental apartments and villas, agriturismos, castles, palaces, boats – many choices! There is no one perfect type of accommodation. What one person loves another doesn't. Choose the type of accommodation that aligns with your travel dreams.

I know people who get the cheapest place possible because they're only going to sleep there and want to use their money for other things. I know other people who have to have 5-star hotels. I have met couch surfers and I have met people doing farm stays. I've stayed in villas and palaces and apartments and bed and breakfasts and cave hotels. I loved everything. Whatever feels comfortable to you is going to be wonderful.

Hotels

I stay in hotels only if the hotel is something really special, or if I will be in a city or town for too few nights to have a vacation rental. To me, most hotel chains all look relatively the same inside. When you wake up in the morning it's hard to know if you are in Spain or in Germany or in Dubuque Iowa. That is not what I want from my Italian vacation. I like a little more character. When I'm on vacation, I want to know exactly where I am the minute I open my eyes. And it needs to feel special. Having said that, there are some absolute hotel jewels to be found! If you are planning on staying in hotels for your trip, spend a little extra time researching.

One of my friends owns an exquisite hotel in **Positano,** the **Hotel Villa Gabrisa.** When you stay there, the moment you open your eyes you know you are in Positano. The rooms are amazing, the views from the huge, private terraces are breathtaking. There are potted lemon trees, gorgeous tiled tables and beautiful chairs on the terraces, adding to the sensational ambience while you enjoy your morning coffee, your room service or your evening glass of wine. It is perfect. Every moment spent in your room or on your private terrace feels special. Villa Gabrisa also has a wonderful restaurant.

In **Matera** I stay in a cave hotel in the Sassi called **le Dodici Lune***. It is spectacular. Centuries-old, it used to be a series of private cave homes built into the side of the hill. The owners acquired this group of homes and refurbished them into a beautiful hotel. They added every modern convenience but kept the hotel true to its history in the Sassi. You wake up in a hotel like this, not only knowing exactly where you are, but knowing that you are in a place so special and unique, you will never ever forget it.

If Matera and the Sassi are not familiar to you, I highly recommend googling them. Matera is one of Italy's best kept secrets. If you have an opportunity to get yourself to there I highly recommend it, even if it is for only one night. In 2019 it will be named the European Capital of Culture.

On the island of **Lipari,** I always stay in the same amazing hotel with terraces and balconies facing the volcanic island of Stromboli. If the volcano goes off I will have the perfect view.

NOT ALL HOTELS HAVE MOD-CONS

Many of the hotels you will come across won't have electronic key cards, and instead use giant old keys that fit into giant old locks in giant old doors. You have to hand your key in at the front desk every time you leave to *go anywhere* and pick up your key when you arrive back. It adds a little old-world charm to the experience.

Some hotels don't have elevators, although those seem to be few and far between these days. If an elevator is important or necessary to you be sure to ask if they have one before booking your hotel.

One of the great things about staying in a hotel in Italy is that they always serve fantastic European breakfasts. I barely eat breakfast at home, but I look forward to it when I'm staying in a hotel in Italy.

Bed & Breakfasts

Normally, staying in a Bed and Breakfast quite literally means you have a bedroom and breakfast in the morning. B&Bs can be in old villas, old apartment-style buildings, castles – you name it!

Some of them are gorgeous. I stayed in one that was part of an old palace in **Sicily's Baroque region**. It was ridiculously beautiful, magical, unique and completely awe-inspiring. We were nearly in tears when we were shown through it. (Okay, I actually did cry.) You could feel the history seeping out of the walls. The passageways and archways and the shapes of the rooms and the staircases all were kept as they were in the early 1700's. Local craftsmen had refurbished everything, from the windows to the doors, to the tile and mosaic floors, exactly as they always were. Every modern addition (including bathrooms, electricity) was done in such a way that it didn't disturb the history of the palace. Waking up there was an experience I will treasure forever.

If you are planning on staying in a B&B you may want to ask if the owners or property managers live in the building. When we stayed at the palace, we were the only people sleeping there. The management company didn't have any employees living onsite. I was totally fine with us having the palace to ourselves, but I know that for some people it may have been a little unnerving. In the future I would probably opt for a B&B that has staff living onsite. The possibility of other guests leaving the front door open or getting wild in the night doesn't sit so well with me.

The downside to staying in a hotel or B&B is that at the end of a long day of sightseeing, you have nowhere to relax except your bed (unless you have a suite), or maybe an upright chair by a little desk in your room. You can't stretch out, lounge around, or get really comfortable unless you stretch out on your bed (and I'm not much a fan of the bed couch).

Rented Rooms

If you are on a tight budget, if you're feeling adventurous, or if you want to immerse yourself in the Italian experience, renting a room in a private home can be a fun option. I have never done it myself but have met plenty of people on my travels who were staying with a family via Airbnb or the like. I've known others who rented a room in a house or apartment where each bedroom was rented out individually.

Vacation Rental – Apartments

This is my favorite type of accommodation. I initially stayed in rental apartments because it cost a fraction of the price of a hotel, and on my single-mommy budget, that was the only way I could afford to travel. I found them by searching websites such as **Airbnb**, **VRBO** and **HomeAway**.

From the moment that I walked into the first apartment I rented, I was hooked. The apartment was on the top floor (the attic) of a 13th century palace in a medieval town in Tuscany. It was beautiful – and still is. I have stayed there every year since and it has become my Italian home. (The owners have become close friends of mine, close enough that they sent their son to live with us in America for a couple of months to practice his English.) I've rented an apartment in a thousand-year-old tower in Lazio; I've rented a modern apartment in Sicily across the street from the beach; I've rented in ancient buildings in Florence and in Rome; I've rented trulli (conical, hobbit looking homes) in Puglia. I have stayed in vacation rentals all over Italy and I have never had an experience that was less than wonderful. And here's why…

WELCOME HOME

Vacation rentals feel homey. At the end of a long day you have a couch to stretch out on, comfortable chairs to hang out in, maybe even a balcony or terrace to chill out on.

One of my Glam Italia women fell in love with the sunflower couch in an apartment in San Gimignano. She had afternoon naps there with the sun streaming in through the window between the towers. She spent evenings there with her book. The hominess of the experience and the opportunity to pretend, just for a minute, that she was part of the life there was far more intoxicating than the wine! When she talks to me about her trip she refers to "living in a centuries-old apartment for a few days", because we really were *living* there rather than just dropping our bags off in a hotel room.

YOUR OWN CUCINA

You have a fully-equipped kitchen, so you can choose to eat some meals at home if you wish. Some people like to eat out every night, but I like eating in sometimes. Why not, when you're surrounded by fresh produce that needs only simple preparation to be incredible!

One of my favorite things to do when I'm in Italy is to shop at the local market, buy fresh fruit and vegetables, prosciutto and local cheeses, breads, olives and wine and have a meal at home. I love stopping at the market and asking the vendors what I should make for dinner that night. They choose the freshest items and then tell me how to prepare them in the way their family has been cooking them for generations. I love interacting with locals on this level, and I feel that it gives me an insight into life in Italy. For a moment I get to pretend that I am part of that life.

I love coming home at the end of the day, making something simple to eat, pouring a glass of wine, stretching out by a window that overlooks an ancient piazza, and alternating between reading my book and watching local life in the town square below. I think that for many of us when we think of traveling in Italy we imagine partaking in the life there for a few days, rather than just whizzing past churches and monuments all day long with a camera and collapsing in a hotel room at night. (I know that is how I imagine it anyway, and so that is the experience I aim to create.)

One last point: eating three meals per day in a restaurant can be exhausting and expensive. You wind up eating more than you want or need, and sometimes after a long day you just want to chill out and relax and not have to go anywhere.

I like having the option to do whatever I feel like each day, and an apartment rental gives me that flexibility.

Vacation Rental – Villas

All the advantages of a vacation rental apartment, but bigger! If you have more people or just want more space, another option in the vacation rental sector is to rent a villa. They are everywhere, and each type of villa creates its own experience.

You will find villas in the countryside, overlooking vineyards or olive groves; there are villas overlooking the ocean, or on the edge of a village; others are right in the heart of town. They always seem to be really old, have sensational history, and to me they are just magic!

I spend a lot of time researching rental villas all over Italy. Often, I just google "vacation rental villas" or "castles" or "palaces" and the region where I want to stay. Some of the really great finds are not on the main vacation rental websites. There are small companies that specialize in high end, exclusive vacation rentals.

If you are going to dream yourself an Italian dream, why not throw in a villa? (Did you know that Sting owns a huge villa in Tuscany, and you can rent it??? Wouldn't that be a scream? "Oh yes I just got back from two weeks in Tuscany. I stayed at Sting's house.")

Castle

Yes, you can rent an entire castle for your vacation, or even just a portion of one. Some have suites available with a bedroom or two, others rent out a whole wing. Whatever your group size, staying in a castle is definitely an option in Italy (believe it, or not!).

Most castles for rent that I have found have been in the countryside, so require you to do some driving. (But can you even imagine your holiday photos?!)

With castles and large villas there is usually an option of having a housekeeper prepare meals for you – either all your meals or some of them. Also, castles and villas tend to have big kitchens and are often well-equipped for on-site cooking lessons, should you want them.

Agriturismo (or Masseria)

An agriturismo is like a farm-stay (agriturismo = agriculture + tourism). These are typically small, boutique farms that don't keep animals. Rather than wallowing with the pigs, you will be strolling through olive groves and vines. Usually, either the main farmhouse is subdivided into apartments or the out-buildings are refurbished into apartments and cottages. This is an ideal option for people who want a quiet, country experience.

My friends Silvana and Piergiorgio own a beautiful agriturismo in the **Crete Senese in Tuscany**, called **Podere Cunina**. Their farmhouse sits on a hill with a view of Montalcino. It is gorgeous, and the sunsets are completely breathtaking. Their guests choose to stay with them so that they can spend their vacation exploring Tuscany. Somedays they drive around finding darling little towns and villages, other days they go on wine tours, and sometimes they just relax and read and go for walks on the property. The agriturismo has olive groves and honey bees. You can buy organic olive oil and honey and saffron to bring home with you (and I always do).

A *masseria*, should you come across the word in your accommodation search, is the name for an agriturismo in southern Italy.

How it Works in a Rental

If you choose to stay in a vacation rental apartment, villa, castle, or agriturismo, they work differently than hotels. There are a few things you need to be aware of:

1. THERE WILL BE NO MAID SERVICE.

No one is going to come and make the beds, take out the trash and clean the bathrooms each day unless you have pre-arranged and paid for a maid. That is not available in most apartments, but you can probably organize it for larger villas and castles (look into it when making your booking).

2. YOU WILL BE CHARGED A CLEANING FEE.

This fee is in addition to the nightly rental cost. In hotels this cost is built in to the price, but in vacation rentals it is a separate charge. (Due to the tax system in Italy, if the cleaning cost is built in to the nightly rate the owner pays up to 55% income tax on it, so instead they treat it as a separate payment that is paid to the cleaning lady.) Apartments seem to average 50 euros for cleaning – some a little more, some less. In any case, the cleaning cost is stipulated when you book your stay, so there should be no surprises. Frequently it is paid in cash.

3. YOU WILL BE CHARGED A SECURITY DEPOSIT IN CASE YOU DAMAGE ANYTHING.

The amount will vary depending on the property you are renting. It will likely be taken at the time of your booking, though is sometimes paid on arrival. If you have booked through an agency or through Airbnb or HomeAway, they will refund your credit card after your stay, once it has been established that no damage was done. If you have booked directly with the owner, they will have stipulated the terms of the refund when you booked with them.

3. YOU WILL PAY TOURIST TAX.

Hotels have this built into their nightly fee, but again private owners of vacation rentals can't really do that. At the time of writing this book, the tourist tax is between 1.50 euros and 3.50 euros per person per night (depending on the region and the city you are staying in). The first time I had to pay it I thought it was a scam. It's not. It's just the system. Tourist tax has to be paid in cash when you arrive.

4. BY LAW YOU HAVE TO SHOW YOUR PASSPORT WHEN YOU CHECK IN.

Whether you are staying in a hotel or a vacation rental, they will either photocopy or write down the details of your passport.

5. THERE ARE DIFFERENT METHODS FOR PAYMENT.

You may be asked to put the deposit on a card but pay the balance in cash when you arrive, or you may be asked to pay in full before you arrive.

6. EUROS OR DOLLARS?

When booking your accommodation, be sure to note whether the price quoted is in euros or in dollars. If it is in euros, you will be getting **the exchange rate of the day you pay it**, not the day you book it. Exchange rates fluctuate, so you could wind up paying much less or much more than anticipated, once it converts to your home currency.

7. ONLY BOOK THROUGH LEGITIMATE AGENCIES.

I don't advise booking directly through an individual, unless you know them. I haven't heard of any scams in Italy with vacation rentals, but it has been a huge problem in Paris and apparently in New York. If you are using a third-party agency, like Airbnb or HomeAway, you have an extra layer of support, and the money is transferred through them, so you have some protection too.

8. CHOOSE A RENTAL WITH LOTS OF REVIEWS (NOT JUST THE BEST REVIEWS).

Even though it might mean missing out on the best place ever, if a rental has no reviews then I'm not going to book it. Let someone else be the first person to try it out.

However, don't dismiss a rental just because it doesn't have five stars. Read through the comments and see what is going on. Sometimes you will see bad reviews written by guests who were expecting hotel service, or by someone who is just trolling. I look to see what threads consistently show up in a series of reviews. If there are multiple reviews saying the area is bad or the water isn't hot or the apartment wasn't clean then I will take that as warning enough not to book it. But if I see a couple of angry reviews alongside multiple happy reviews, I will pay more attention to the happy folks.

One of my all-time favorite rental apartments in Rome, where I have not only repeatedly stayed myself but has also been rented by friends and family on my recommendation, has three bad reviews. It also has 65+ fantastic reviews, some of which are mine! It was the consistent reviews saying the place was great, the beds were cozy, the landlady was lovely, and the location was fantastic that sold me on the place. (If I had listened to the haters I would have missed out on a really incredible apartment.)

9. KNOW THAT IT PROBABLY WON'T BE WHAT YOU'RE USED TO.

Depending on where you are, rooms may be small, and beds may be narrow (you frequently see single beds – remember to check the bed configuration so you know what to expect). Most of these buildings

are centuries old and won't be having walls torn out to make bigger bedrooms for tourists. It is part of the charm!

10. PLAN ON CLIMBING A LOT OF STAIRS.

Many of these buildings will not have elevators, so be prepared to climb a lot of stairs! Often these staircases are narrow and steep. Factor this in when you are planning your luggage because *you* will be the person dragging it up those stairs! (There's no doorman or porter in a vacation rental.) I learned this lesson the hard way, by dragging a heavy suitcase *and* a carry-on bag up multiple flights of stairs. It was miserable! (And I didn't wear half the clothes I had brought with me, so all that heavy lifting was for nothing.)

If you have physical limitations that would make dealing with stairs too difficult or too exhausting, make sure you factor this into your search. Look for buildings with elevators or rent only ground floor apartments. Make sure you ask the owner if there is an elevator prior to making your booking.

11. BOOK YOUR ACCOMMODATION AS SOON AS POSSIBLE.

Italy is a popular vacation destination and accommodation books up fast – especially the best places.

12. TOWELS.

In America, hotels and vacation rentals tend to have stacks of towels. In Italy, for the most part, expect one towel per person. If you need more then bring one with you. Also, they don't have wash cloths. If you use wash cloths, then bring a couple from home. I always bring a couple, plus a large zip-lock bag in case they are still damp when I am packing.

13. BYO TOILET PAPER.

When you stay in a vacation rental there will be toilet paper rolls in the apartment when you arrive, but it is up to you to buy more as you need them. There may be soaps and toiletries on hand, but don't count on it.

14. WRITE A REVIEW FOR YOUR LANDLORD/HOST.

Reviews are crucial to their business. My experience renting apartments in Italy is extensive. I have rented vacation rental apartments, villas and properties all over Italy and Sicily for years and years and I have never had a bad one. In my experience, landlords have always been incredibly friendly and readily available to me by phone or WhatsApp when I need help. (I always need help figuring out the washing machine.). They have ordered private cars to take me to the airport, have recommended places to eat and things to do and have been part of a really fabulous experience. Many of them have even become great friends.

Choosing A Neighborhood

My first rule with big cities is to avoid anywhere near the train station. The area around Santa Maria Novella station in Florence (a small city) is fine, but the area around Termini station in Rome, not so much. Big city train stations tend to attract the less desirables, and although there are exceptions to every rule, I prefer to avoid the risk. I also avoid staying near a major tourist site, largely because it will be more expensive and will probably have more issues with crowds and noise.

When I am going to a town for the first time, I prepare by doing my research. I look at a map to see where everything is, factor in transport – do I have to drive to and from this area or is it walking distance from everywhere? Is it close to public transport? Sometimes I find really incredible places to stay, but they are too far out or too difficult to get to, so I keep looking. I like places where I can walk down the street to get coffee and where there are nice places to eat nearby.

You can find out a lot about an area by reading reviews. I usually start with TripAdvisor and then follow up with reading reviews on hotels and vacation rentals nearby. You might find a fabulous-looking hotel or vacation rental but when you read the reviews, you learn that it is really noisy or backs onto an alley full of trash or is down the street from something undesirable.

You might discover a fantastic new area by stumbling onto a hotel or apartment that looks good, and then through reading the reviews find that there is loads to do nearby, the transport is great, and the neighborhood is wonderful. (I have found some of my favorite neighborhoods this way!) Other travelers writing about their experiences is a great way not only to learn about great areas to stay in but also to find out things to do in the area that may not be in the guide books!

I make an effort to write reviews everywhere I go because I find other peoples' reviews so helpful when I am the one going somewhere new. If you have a great experience somewhere, take the time to write a quick review. You will not only be helping the business, but also other travelers planning their trips.

Bookings, Airport Tricks & Traveling Tips

CHAPTER FOUR
Booking Your Flights

Know where to look

You've chosen your travel dates, you know where in Italy you want to go, you possibly even have your itinerary mapped out. Now it's time to book your flights.

This can be the most stressful part of your entire trip, so I am going to walk you through some fabulous travel hacks, show you how to get a great price on your ticket, and fill you in on a few crucial details about flying in and out of Italy.

Crossing the Dateline

For those of you traveling from the US, for the most part you need to book your flight departure for the day prior to the day you want to arrive. For example, if your trip starts on 4 April and you are taking a direct flight to Italy, you will need to depart the US on 3 April.

Most direct flights from the US leave in the late afternoon or early evening and arrive in Italy the following morning. Direct flights returning to the US generally arrive the same day as they leave. For example, if you depart Rome on 20 April and fly to JFK airport in New York, you will also arrive at JFK on 20 April.

Early Morning Departures from Italy to the US

Another thing item to factor into your flight equation if **flying direct from Italy to the US,** is that all direct flights to the US depart Italy by noon each day.

At the time of writing this, there is a second layer of security screening for direct flights to the US, so you need to allow extra time at the airport before your flight. When multiple airlines have flights to America departing within the same hour, the lines at this second security can take a *really long time*.

It can be difficult to get from one city to another in Italy in time for that early morning flight, unless you are paying a driver a small fortune to drive you. When booking your flight home, be aware that it's wise to stay in the city of departure the night before you leave.

FOR EXAMPLE... FROM ROME TO THE US (STARTING IN POSITANO)

If you are staying in Positano but your flight to the US is departing from Rome at 11am, the only way to get to the airport in Rome by 8:30–9am to check in and go through security is to have a driver pick you up at your hotel or villa around 3:30am and drive you to Rome. This normally costs around 450–500 euros. Or you can stay in Rome for the final night of your trip and take a cab or private driver to the airport for 50 euros.

So, if you are traveling with three or four others it would make sense to have a driver bring you from Positano. They all drive Mercedes minivans, which are super comfortable on long rides, and at a mere

100 or so euros each it's probably a better deal than booking a hotel in Rome.

FOR EXAMPLE... FROM MILAN TO THE US (STARTING IN FLORENCE)

If you are staying in Florence but flying home on a direct flight from Milan, the only way to get you to the airport on time for an early check in is to hire a private driver. Flights from Florence to Milan don't depart early enough, and train service from Florence to Milan begins too late to get you there on time, so if you're travelling in a group your best bet is to stay in Milan or somewhere nearby the night before you leave.

Italy To & From Other Destinations

If you are flying to another European city or through Great Britain, your departing flight will frequently leave later in the day, making the equation for the final night of your vacation easier. Flights out of Italy going to Munich or Dublin or Stockholm for example, may leave after midday, giving you ample time to catch a train from wherever you are to your departure city.

If you are flying to Italy from Asia, Australia, New Zealand, South Africa etc. chances are you have a *really long flight ahead*! I sincerely recommend breaking up your journey to Italy. I have flown from New Zealand to Europe without a break in the past and it is a long, *long* trip. You can brave it and do it in one long stretch, but you may find your first few days in Italy are claimed by jetlag. (My first trip from New Zealand to London was 36 hours across Asia. I did it in one long stretch and it took days to shake off the jetlag.)

If you are traveling trans-world and can swing an overnight somewhere enroute it can give you a chance to walk around a new city, stretch your legs and see something new. Some of my Glam Italia women have had layovers in Dublin, Munich, Brussels, Stockholm, and Istanbul, that allowed them to experience a new city for a few hours. They had a great time and arrived in Italy ready to take on the world.

The Importance of Time

BEWARE SHORT LAYOVERS AND SHORT CONNECTIONS

If you have the great fortune to live in a city with an airport that has direct flights to Italy, you won't have to deal with layovers. For the rest of us, the layover is something to factor into the equation.

The first type of layover that I want you to be careful with is the short layover, or short connection. Most airlines have one international flight to Italy per day per airport, so if you miss your connecting flight you can be waiting 24 hours to catch the next one, assuming there is an open seat on that next flight.

In all my years flying from the US to Italy, I have found that all flights seem to depart within a few hours of one another, regardless of the airline, so if you miss your flight to Rome departing out of Detroit you won't have time to get to Philly to catch a flight from there.

Things happen, planes run late. Any time I have had a connection of two hours or less it has been pure luck that has had me boarding my international flight on time, not wily cleverness. If you have a short turn-around-time, the chances of your bag getting from your domestic flight to your international flight are slimmer too.

Then there is the issue of getting across the airport from the arrival gate to the gate you are departing from. A smaller airport like Charlotte NC is doable at high speed, but some of the larger airports require that you exit the secure area, consequently forcing you to go back through security, which can in turn make you miss your connecting flight. Some airports require you to go to an entirely different terminal for international departures and arrivals, so do your research to ensure the logistics are manageable before buying your ticket.

LEAVE ENOUGH TIME TO CLEAR CUSTOMS

Also factor this in for the return flight: **when you land in your final destination country, you have to clear customs before going to your connecting domestic flight.** Some international airports are incredibly functional and well-organized, like Sydney airport. They employ smiling, friendly people who can handle multiple large-load planes arriving at the same time and get the people and the bags moved through expeditiously. Others, not so much.

When you have a connecting domestic flight after your international flight, you will usually clear customs and then recheck your bags at the transfer desk outside of the customs hall. This is especially easy and functional when your connecting flight is with the same airline or with one of their partner carriers. Some airports are set up so that you can clear customs, recheck your bag and go to your next flight without having to exit and come back through security. However, most airports in the US make you go back through security, which can make even a reasonable length layover too short.

I frequently fly back from Italy into New York JFK airport – it's always a nightmare. When you're already exhausted, not only do you have to exit and go back in through security, but the lines can be long, and the workers unfriendly. While waiting in line, I've found myself wondering whether their job description included: *"must dislike people, have a miserable outlook on life, specialize in jackassery and have a gargantuan chip on shoulder. Smiling, friendly people will not be considered."* ...So anyway, make sure you have **at least** **three hours layover** between arriving at JFK and catching your domestic flight.

LONG LAYOVERS AREN'T SO BAD

A long layover is not necessarily a bad thing. It can give you an opportunity to explore a new city for a few hours. One of my friends had a 12-hour layover in Munich on her way from Los Angeles to Cape Town, so she put her suitcase in a locker and went into town. She walked around, saw some sights, did some window shopping – Munich is a great city in which to wander around aimlessly. She had a wonderful meal in town and got back to the airport with plenty of time to collect her bags and check in for her next flight. She arrived in Cape Town feeling relaxed and not too worn out, whereas had she only had a 4-hour layover she would have arrived feeling exhausted.

Note: *Check the airport you are flying into to see what their rules are regarding luggage and long layovers. Most airports have a rule that you have to collect your luggage and recheck it if your layover is more than a set number of hours. Some airports it's 8 hours, some it's 12, so make sure you check first. You may not be able to check your bag back in for your next flight for several hours, so if you are going into town during your layover, you may need to leave your suitcase in a locker. Do a little extra research ahead of time to see if the airport has them.*

IN-TERMINAL HOTELS

Airports like Singapore Changi have in-terminal hotels where you can stop overnight or even for just a few hours to sleep, shower and break up that long trek. You don't actually leave the terminal, so you don't have to go through security again, and don't have to figure out getting transport to a hotel offsite.

I have used **Yotel at London Heathrow Airport** and both the **Yotel and Hotel Mercure in Amsterdam's Schiphol** when I have had a ten-hour, overnight layover. The concept of a hotel inside the airport that you can book for just a few hours is fantastic!

REALLY LONG LAYOVERS

Many consolidators (websites like Travelocity, Orbitz and Expedia, which offer flights from multiple airlines) offer cheap flights with really long layovers. Look at them and see if the savings are worthwhile. Often the layovers have you sitting inside the terminal overnight or require that you get a hotel if the airport won't let you wait there. Once you've factored in the cost of meals, drinks, accommodation, transport to and from a hotel, and the general discomfort of hanging around inside a terminal for hours on end, it can end up costing you more than you think you are saving.

I recently helped two of my Glam Italia women book their airline tickets. Their flight home routed them back through Toronto where they had a 17-hour layover. Even once we factored in a hotel room for the night, they still saved a combined $800 on the two round trip airfares, so it was well worth it. We discarded loads of flights that initially seemed like a great price but they had layovers in cities that made it too expensive when the external costs were added in, or they had awkward layovers on the inbound flight that would have had them arriving in Italy feeling jetlagged beyond belief.

If you are traveling internationally for the first time, I recommend streamlining your flight as much as possible. Try to choose the simplest flight with the fewest connections and layovers, even if it does cost a little more. Ideally, book a flight that goes directly from your hometown to the departure city, rather than buying a deal with multiple domestic legs. My American readers may be familiar with discount flights flying through 3 cities across the country before arriving at your departure city. These flight plans, although cheaper by a couple of hundred dollars, are exhausting and if this is your first international flight you may end up completely overwhelmed by it all.

I always think the fewer times you have to change planes, the less likely your luggage will get lost enroute. And I am all about having my suitcase arrive when I do!

LAYOVERS, TOILETRIES AND SECURITY IN HEATHROW

If you're planning a layover, then you'll want to pack a few toiletries in your carry-on bag. One word of warning: if you are flying through London's Heathrow Airport, they have a smaller carry-on allowance for toiletries than in any other international airport I have used in the past 20+ years. They give you a small, sandwich-sized zip-lock bag when you are going through X-ray, and anything that doesn't fit inside it goes in the trash. That includes mascara, lipstick, any non-powder makeup items – even travel-sized toothpaste! I have traveled round and round the world with the exact same carry-on toiletry and makeup bags, with the same tried and trusted items in them, and this was the only time they have been taken from me. So be careful with Heathrow!

Airline Travel Hacks

You know how to plan your travel dates, you've considered your connections and layovers, now let's look at some great travel hacks to help you find a less expensive flight.

FREQUENT FLIER MILES

People always ask me how I can keep taking international trips on a single-mom income. The answer is that I have mastered the art of the frequent flier mile.

Years ago, I started accruing frequent flier miles on my credit card. I didn't get an airline credit card, but instead I chose a card that lets me use any airline I want. In the US, American Express, the Barclay Card group and Capital One all have cards with fantastic frequent flier programs. (Many of these cards also have no international fees, so they're helpful to have while you are away.)

I started using my card like a debit card. I paid every transaction and every bill I possibly could with my credit card, earning one or two miles per dollar along the way. I would then move the money over from my checking account, paying my card off each day, so that I never had a balance owing (and I never overspent!). It is amazing how much money we spend on bills, groceries, filling up the car, and doing everyday things. Those frequent flier miles keep growing each month!

Cards like American Express or Capital One don't have blackout days and they work with most airlines. A round trip from the US to Europe costs around 50,000 frequent flier miles, so it doesn't take long to build up sufficient miles for a free trip! Of course, it's not entirely free – there are airport departure taxes, so depending on which airports you are using the round trip costs somewhere in the vicinity of $350.

When I am not using miles to book my flight, I am double dipping. I accrue miles with the airline that I am flying, but I also earn even more miles by booking the flight with my credit card. The cards I use give me two miles per $1 spent on air travel. The miles add up quickly.

If I am using frequent flier miles for my trip, securing my flight is the first thing I work on. A given flight may not have "non-revenue" seats available on the day I want to go, so I may have to change my travel plans a day or two to either side. To me it has always been worth it, and I have flown back and forth many, many times on frequent flier miles!

INCOGNITO WINDOW

This trick is important. Open an incognito window (or private search) on your computer every time you are looking for flights. **Airlines and consolidators track you when you start searching flights, then start raising the price as they see you come back.** One of their tactics is to start telling you *there are only 3 seats left at this price*! If you use incognito windows to do your searching they can't track you, and you will see better deals popping up.

A perfect example of this was when I was recently helping a traveler from one of my tours find flights. She had been looking already, so the consolidators and airlines were tracking her. While on the phone together, on the same website, looking at the exact same flight, at the exact same time, her screen was quoting $1390 while mine was quoting $872. The incognito window will save you money!

GOOGLE FLIGHTS

If you have flexible dates, Google Flights can be your best friend. Put your approximate flight dates and your flight stop and start points (like Phoenix to Florence) and see which days of the week or month have the lowest-fares. You can save hundreds of dollars by going a day earlier or staying a day later.

If you have a tour booked, you won't be able to be quite so flexible, but you still may be able to save hundreds of dollars by arriving a day early or departing a day later. This morning I was looking at flights to New Zealand from Los Angeles, and by changing the departure by two days the price went from $1500 each way to $812. Big difference.

CONSOLIDATOR SEARCH VS AIRLINE SEARCH

Initially start with the consolidators and see the types of deals they are offering, so you know at what point the prices are averaging. Different consolidators work with different airlines, so check more than one. I love **Momondo**, but I also check **Expedia, Orbitz** and **Travelocity**.

Once you have an idea of the average price, look on the airlines' websites to see how they compare, and if they can offer better deals. Sometimes I call the airline and have them help me. They find me deals that beat what I'm seeing online, because they know clever ways to re-route the trip.

Routing your Flights

LOOK INTO DEPARTING FROM NEARBY AIRPORTS

Starting with your home airport, check the flight prices and then compare them to the cost of starting your flight at a nearby airport instead. Most of the time I can save hundreds of dollars by starting my flight in Los Angeles instead of Phoenix. When I flew to Paris in May of 2017 it cost me $700 less to start my flight in Los Angeles rather than in Phoenix. The cost of a separate Phoenix to Los Angeles flight was only $50. Then, after finding that price online, I called the airline (Delta) and they were able to match the deal, ***and*** route me a return flight from Rome to JFK and then directly into Phoenix (instead of back to Los Angeles), which saved me another $50.

I have had other international flights that have been markedly cheaper if I routed them out of Tucson. Check out your options and see if it benefits you to start your trip from another airport.

LOOK INTO ARRIVING INTO NEARBY AIRPORTS

Then the next thing to do is to look at your airport options at the other end. Sometimes it's cheaper to fly into Milan than Rome. Sometimes you can get a smoking hot deal on a flight into Florence rather than to Rome or Milan. When you open up your options you can sometimes save a substantial amount of money. Some cities (such as Milan) have more than one airport. You may find a flight into Milan Linate for less than a flight into Milan Malpensa or vice versa.

As I've already mentioned, the train system in Italy is easy to use, inexpensive and extremely efficient, so if you take a flight into a different city than originally planned it is easy to jump on a train and get to where you want to be. (More on trains later.)

LOOK INTO ARRIVING INTO NEARBY COUNTRIES

If your flight directly into Italy is looking expensive, check the prices to fly into a different European city. You can sometimes find a cheaper option by flying into another city, such as Munich or Dublin, sometimes even Paris! Generally internal flights within Europe are quite affordable. I have flown to Italy through Paris many times, especially if I'm starting my Italian trip in Florence.

The Multi City Option

When searching for flights you will have the option to select one-way or return. There is another option available too – multi city.

A multi city flight option allows you to fly into one city and out of another. Sometimes this can make your trip easier as you don't have to organize additional transport within the country you are flying to.

FOR EXAMPLE...

If your trip is starting on the Amalfi Coast and ending in Rome, your round-trip option would be flying in and out of Rome. Your multi city option might be to fly **into** Naples and **out of** Rome. If you fly round-trip to Rome then on arrival you will have to take the express train from the airport to Termini station, then another train from Termini to Naples. It is quite easy to do but if you are exhausted from your long flight it can add a layer of stress to your arrival. Using the option of flying into Naples instead may be both cheaper and more efficient.

Many of my Glam Italia tours start in Florence and end in Rome. My travelers typically get multi city flight options that route them in to Florence and out of Rome. If they fly into Rome then they have to cover the additional cost of the train trip to Florence (plus the round-trip train fare for me to come up and get them).

When I am researching my own flights I always look at the multi city options as well as the round-trip options. Sometimes there is no difference in price, sometimes there is a huge difference in price, and sometimes it is just very much more convenient!

Daylight

I always like to arrive during daylight hours, even in cities that I know well. If there is an unbelievable deal on a flight that has me arriving at night I normally won't take it. If there are any problems between the airport and the hotel or vacation rental, or with the check-in at a hotel or vacation rental, I would rather that happen in daylight! (I have never had a problem when arriving in Italy, but I prefer to play it safe.)

Premium Economy, Economy, or Basic Economy?

Depending on the plane configuration, your flight may offer any combination of Premium Economy, Economy and Basic Economy seating. (If you are flying Business or First class, consider yourself blessed and you can skip this part!)

All flights offer Economy and depending on the airline it can be fantastic (for example Emirates and Air New Zealand). There are other airlines with economy classes that are not so good, so again, do some research.

Premium Economy costs more but is generally a worthwhile choice. You get a larger seat and more leg room, often with a foot bar to raise your legs, which really makes it worth spending the extra! Premium gets a better menu, better service, has larger screens to watch movies on, and is sectioned off at the front of the economy section. On Dreamliners, Premium Economy is often upstairs, which is also pretty fabulous.

Basic Economy can mean different things on different flights. Check the details for the flight you are considering. It *can* mean no overhead bin, or only one small piece of carry-on luggage that can fit under the seat in front of you. It *can* mean you pay for luggage and it *can* mean you don't get food included or inflight entertainment. Basic Economy doesn't include choosing your seat, doesn't give you frequent flyer benefits, and has you boarding your flight in the last boarding group. So far there doesn't seem to be an industry standard for what Basic Economy entails, and each airline has its own variation.

I recently flew standby to Paris on American Airlines and was put in an Economy seat. The people in the row behind me had paid $500 each for a Basic Economy round-trip ticket but didn't have any restrictions put on them at all – there was no difference between what regular economy got and what they got. Other times I hear people say that everything is an upcharge, even drinks and meals.

Selecting Your Seat

Once you have your flight booked you should select your seat on the plane. If you don't take an active part in organizing your seat assignment you will wind up in the dreaded middle seat. Trust me – if you have to pay extra to select your seat, do it. If I am flying First class or Business class I don't care where they seat me – it's going to be fabulous regardless. If you have purchased a Basic Economy seat you may not have this option at all.

If I am flying Premium Economy or Economy I like to have a window seat. With a window seat I have a wall to lean against and am not impacted by other people's bathroom schedules. Some of my friends swear by aisle seats, but I find that if I eventually manage to fall asleep sitting upright, I either get woken up almost immediately by someone in my row needing to go to the toilet, or I get banged in the head by someone walking down the aisle with a bag in their hand.

I use an app called **SeatGuru** to help me choose my seat. Assuming you are flying in the main cabin in one of the economy classes, SeatGuru is an invaluable tool to have at your disposal. Not all seats are created equal. Some are too close to the toilets, others have an entertainment unit under the seat in front of you, preventing you from stretching your legs or stashing your bag within reach. Some seats don't recline, or are super narrow or unpadded, others have no seat at all in front and require all bags to be stored in the overhead bin. I use SeatGuru every time I fly. It has saved me from a bad seat numerous times!

CHAPTER FIVE
Airport Hacks

Keep your airport game strong

I am a big believer that the key to having a great flight and arriving at your destination feeling good (or at least not feeling beaten up and looking like hell) is in your preparation and your airport game. You need to keep your airport game strong.

Airport Food

Most airports have really unhealthy food options. Airport food is generally overpriced, high sodium, high fat, high carb – basically the exact opposite of what you should be eating prior to an international flight.

Fortunately, there are some exceptions: **Los Angeles LAX** airport has some great, healthy food options such as Real Food and Earth Bar, **Seattle's SEA-TAC** airport has fresh sushi, **Phoenix Sky Harbor** has Le Grand Orange. There are many more airports with good food options, but most of the good food is hard to find, being eclipsed by fast food and super processed food. To address this, one of the best things you can do is plan ahead and pack healthy snacks to tide you over at the airport. This will also save you a fortune, because airport food is notoriously expensive. Avoid salty snacks. Salty food can cause swelling and fluid retention. Heavy food can make you feel uncomfortable during your flight, so you are better to eat lightly. Opt instead for fresh fruit, vegetables (but not cruciferous vegetables) unsalted nuts, cheese, and protein bars.

I suggest bringing an empty water bottle and filling it at a water station once you go through the security checkpoint. A full bottle of water will be confiscated if you attempt to take it through security and bottled water is expensive if you buy it at the airport. However you do it, make sure you have a large bottle of water with you when boarding your flight. It is essential to drink lots of water throughout the flight to help offset jetlag, dehydration and headaches.

Utilize Airport Amenities

Some airports have really cool amenities that you can take advantage of to break up the monotony of a long layover, or to make your next flight more pleasant. From karaoke bars to day spas to free movie theaters showing current movies, if you are lucky enough to be routed through a super user-friendly airport, make use of the options available to you!

By the time I arrive at the airport to fly to Italy, I am always exhausted. No matter how hard I try, I always end up having to work until the last minute. When I finally buckle up on my flight I am so tired I can barely see straight. (I am also pre-programmed to avoid short connection times for international flights, so I've spent a lot of time waiting in airports.) So, my favorite thing to do while waiting for my international flight to depart is to go to one of the **chair massage spas** that now seem to be in almost every international terminal. They are overpriced compared to non-airport spas but there is huge value in having a 20-minute shoulder, neck and back massage before or after a long flight. Unless you are flying in Business class or

First class, flying puts a strain on your body. It's not always particularly comfortable, and your neck and shoulders bear a lot of that burden. Having someone work over your neck and shoulders can be a game-changer before a long flight. If nothing else it's a great way to kill time!

Airline Lounges

Depending on your airline, you may be able to buy a day pass into their club lounge. They all seem to have different rules. Air New Zealand only allows Koru Club members and Business and First class passengers to use their Koru Lounge. American Airlines let you buy a $50-daypass, regardless of your seat status.

LoungeBuddy is an app I use to research the lounges at airports I'm flying through, to see if it is worthwhile paying to use them or not. Some airport lounges are wonderful, others just marginal. LoungeBuddy lets you buy day passes to lounges in airports all around the world, so if you're flying with American Airlines it may be possible to buy a day pass into the Lufthansa lounge (if American doesn't have one).

WHEN IT'S WORTH USING A CLUB LOUNGE

I think it is only worth it if you have a long layover. At the time of writing this, I am preparing to take a redeye from Phoenix to Miami. I depart Phoenix at 1am, arrive in Miami at 7am, and depart Miami for Barcelona at around 6pm. I am flying American Airlines, so I am planning to use their club lounge during the 11 hours I have to kill at the airport in Miami.

In the lounge, I will be able to have a shower, freshen up and change my clothes. The club lounge has big leather chairs with coffee tables and charging stations, so I can spend the day working on my computer, relaxing in comfort (which is HUGE compared to sitting for hours in the terminal). There is good WiFi, which is important if you have work to do or want to watch movies. The restroom facilities are modern and clean. There are complimentary snacks, soups and salads, fruits and drinks available all day, as well as a small restaurant where you can order larger meals if you feel so inclined. The restaurant meals are not free, but they tend to offer options unavailable in the terminal restaurants, and the convenience makes it worthwhile. I normally find the complimentary food is all I need. They offer enough variety throughout the day to keep it interesting and the food options tend to be relatively healthy and lightweight. Using the club lounge can make a big difference when you have a long layover.

If you buy a day pass with American Airlines you can use it at multiple airports that day. When my son was young we would use the club lounge in Phoenix prior to our flight, then use the club lounge in Charlotte for the hours of layover we had there before flying to Rome. It made the trip so much easier and we would board our international flight feeling relaxed. I can't recommend it enough!

What to Wear on Your Flight

When I fly, my ultimate goal is to get upgraded. I also want to be comfortable and warm. These things direct my wardrobe choices for any flight. I will get to the upgrade part later, but for now let's talk about comfort and warmth (and self-respect!).

Showing up for a flight in pyjamas (it happens), sweats, or any outfit that is too casual looks plain awful. The same goes for hot pants, micro minis and anything else along that line. When planning your outfit for a long-haul flight, your first priority should be comfort – but that should not be your only priority!

Look for wardrobe choices that are not constricting and fabrics that breathe and move with you. You will be sitting for hours on end, the seat may not be comfortable, and your body may swell. (Even the most seasoned flyer can experience unexpected swelling!) Wearing clothing that is too fitted or that cuts you in half (like jeans) can make you miserable. You also have to factor in temperature – it may be cold on the plane, warm or hot in the airport, and the climates that you are departing from and arriving into may differ dramatically.

Your best bet is to layer loose fitting (but chic!) items in dark colors and natural fabrics (like bamboo, cotton or merino). I have a travel uniform that I have used for years. It works like a dream and gets me upgraded often. My travel uniform is all black, partly because black looks chic with little to no effort, and partly because it hides creases and any unplanned spills better than color does. I wear palazzo/boot cut pants that have a matching loose fit tank and a matching loose fit, stylish, long-sleeved, asymmetrical top. Heels are not a good idea when you are flying, so I wear flats. I also carry a pashmina that I can use as an oversized scarf, or as a blanket if I get cold on the plane. The fabrics all breathe, are lightweight, cool when it's hot and seem to keep the chill off when it's cool. I don't arrive looking wrinkled and disheveled, and the slight swish to the leg of the pants makes the outfit look fresh when I deplane.

Another super important component of your flying outfit is the addition of compression socks or hose. Regardless of your age or weight, I heartily recommend compression legwear! They prevent swelling of the feet and ankles. The medical grade compression stops fluid from pooling in your lower extremities, which seems to lessen the exhausting effects of flying, but also has been proven to be effective in the prevention of DVT (Deep Vein Thrombosis).

Most people take their shoes off during the flight. If you are likely to take your shoes off I recommend bringing a pair of cheap socks to put on over your compression hose. Airplanes are dirty, even when they are clean. If you use the restroom you need to either put your shoes on or be wearing socks that you can throw away at the end of the flight. Personally, I won't go near an airplane bathroom without shoes on. (Just so you know, those wet drops on the floor probably aren't water....)

Getting Upgraded

I have the upgrade down to a fine art and it's not complicated. You can pay for an upgrade, use frequent flier miles or sometimes get it for free. It's all about being nice!

Airlines frequently sell out the economy section, or even oversell flights. Often Business or First class have some vacant seats, which means there is an opportunity to move up. If you are smiling and friendly, (look around you – most people in the airport are just the opposite), if you look stylish, and are in the right place at the right time you may find yourself getting upgraded.

When I am checking in I always ask the agent if the flight is full. I have been upgraded at check in before, but more frequently it happens later in the process. If they tell me the flight is full, my next stop is the gate agent (who holds all the power in this equation). I let them know straight up that if they have to upgrade anyone I would like to be considered!

Most airlines won't allow you to be upgraded if you are wearing jeans, even if they are the most expensive jeans on the market. They want to make sure the person they are upgrading *looks and behaves* appropriately. Therefore, **I make sure that I'm dressed suitably and that I am the one person in the waiting area who is smiling and friendly**, no matter how tired I am feeling.

I recently flew from Los Angeles to Paris and asked the woman at check in if the flight was full. While in line I noticed that everyone around me looked moody or disinterested, and some already looked disheveled and frazzled. I on the other hand was wearing my trusty travel uniform and was thrilled to be on my way to Paris, so I looked stylish and happy. When I asked if the flight was full, she cryptically asked if I was hoping to upgrade. I said I would love that, as long as it wasn't expensive. She went and talked to her supervisor, who looked me up and down and whispered to her. She came back and told me I could be upgraded for $300. I figured why not? She told me she had to escort me to the other line and waited with me so that she could hand me off to the next agent. The agent she passed me to was also super friendly. I told him I was excited to be upgraded because I had just spent three months working seven days per week and was beyond exhausted. He hit a button on his computer and said, "Oh look! The price just went down, now it's only $200". I was thrilled to pieces and told him so. He hit the button again and said, "Now its $87!" Long story short, I paid $87 extra and rode at the front of the plane!

Another time when I was flying home from Milan, I had asked the gate agent if there were going to be any upgrades available and she told me no, the flight was full. I noticed there were standbys hoping to get on the flight, so asked her if a First/Business class passenger didn't show up could she move me up and sell my seat to a standby customer. A short while later I was buckled into my Economy class seat, my carry-on in the overhead bin, waiting for the flight to depart, when she walked straight down the aisle to me with one of the standby passengers behind her. She said, "Ms Cooke, can you please come with me?" and escorted me to the front of the plane to a seat in Business class.

I frequently (though of course not always) get upgraded on international flights. I am convinced that it all comes down to being dressed nicely, smiling at the ground staff, and having a great attitude!

CHAPTER SIX
What to Pack in Your Carry-on Bag

Be prepared!

Having a strong game plan with your carry-on bag is really important. On your flight to Italy, your carry-on bag needs to have items you may need during your flight as well as items to keep you going should your suitcase not arrive with you. I give all my Glam Italia travelers this advice and I'm giving it to you too.

Most of the time your suitcase will arrive in Italy on the same airplane that you do. Other times it won't. One of my travelers in 2017 got separated from her suitcase at JFK in New York. She boarded a flight to Rome and her suitcase went to Boston. Then Amsterdam. Then somewhere else in Europe. Then La Guardia in New York. She was reunited with her suitcase on Day 8 of her 11-day tour. Unfortunately for her, she hadn't bothered to read my email about what to pack in her carry-on and didn't have so much as a toothbrush with her!

One of my friends took a three-week trip to Spain and had to live out of her carry-on bag for the entire trip when the airline lost her suitcase. It doesn't happen often, *but occasionally it does happen.*

Touch wood, my suitcase has always arrived with me, but in the event that it doesn't arrive, I'm not going to ruin my trip by not being prepared. I always pack three days' worth of clothes, toiletries and makeup in my carry-on bag. If my suitcase does get separated from me I at least can change my outfit and I figure I can just keep washing clothes every couple of days until it does arrive.

Consider what you'll need:

1. THREE DAYS' WORTH OF CLOTHES, TOILETRIES AND MEDICATIONS

I plan three days' worth of easy-to-pack, interchangeable, mix and match items that work with the shoes I am traveling in. It's not as impossible as it sounds. It can be as simple as a pair of pants, a skirt and three tops, as well as something to sleep in and some underwear. I roll everything and pack it into a medium-sized packing cube within my carry-on. (Packing cubes are zippered rectangular pouches that stack evenly in your suitcase and make packing and staying organized while you are traveling so much easier! I use Eagle Creek packing cubes.) So, all that stuff doesn't take up much space. Italians don't use wash cloths, so I always pack one of those in my carry-on too, along with toiletries in 3 ounce/100ml bottles.

Make sure you put any medications you regularly take in your carry-on bag.

2. JEWELRY AND TECHNOLOGY

I don't recommend bringing expensive jewelry with you, but if you feel compelled to do so, pack it in your carry-on, *not your suitcase*. Your iPad or laptop should be in your carry-on along with any expensive camera equipment. In a small packing cube, I carry my power adaptors, phone charger and charging cords. I also carry two fully-charged external phone batteries with me when I fly (keep reading to find out why!)

3. CREATURE COMFORTS

The final items to get packed into my carry-on bag are my pashmina, some snacks, and a zip-lock bag with a packet of antibacterial wipes and a packet of wet wipes.

4. WIPES

You need to be able to clean your hands whenever necessary, so a small pack of baby wipes come in really handy. Use your antibacterial wipes to disinfect the surrounding surfaces when you first find your seat. Wipe down the arm rests, the seat belt buckle, the tray table (people change babies diapers on the same tray table your book, snacks, drink and meal will later be sitting on!) the head rest, and if you have a window seat and are likely to rest your head against the wall, wipe that down too. My flight attendant friend tells me never to use the seat pocket in front of you because passengers blow their noses and then put the tissues in there. If you are planning on storing belongings in the seat pocket be sure to try to clean down the inside first.

5. SNACKS

During your flight you will usually be served a meal and have snacks available to you. I think it is a good idea to have some protein bars and other healthy, non-salty snacks in your bag just in case you get stuck somewhere along the way. You hear about planes being parked on the tarmac for hours or being re-routed to a random airport overnight because a traveler got sick, and the remaining passengers having no access to food or drink. In all my years of flying round and round the world it has never happened to me, but I do like to be prepared.

6. EYE DROPS, NASAL SPRAY, COUGH DROPS

I always fly with a small bottle of eye drops, a small nasal spray and some cough drops. The air in the plane on a long-haul flight is very dry. Having dry scratchy eyes would be really annoying and I have heard of people getting sinus pain while flying. I sometimes get a dry cough on a plane (or worry that I will get one), so I always have cough drops with me.

What kind of carry-on bag?

For a long time, I used a soft, duffel style carry-on so that once I landed I could transfer everything into my suitcase and have only one bag to drag around. That changed after reading a post by a travel writer who flew into Istanbul airport right before a bomb went off. Sure, the chances of you being in an airport that is under a terrorist attack or a major weather event are negligible, and I personally don't have any fear of something like that happening, but neither did the writer of the post. She flew for a living, was always somewhere exciting, and thought she had her travel game down. Then the Istanbul event happened. It changed her carry-on plan forever, and by extension, mine too.

The things she talked about in her article included having a carry-on with 360-degree wheels, because she'd had to walk miles to get out of the airport and to a hotel. (There were no taxis or buses allowed into the airport area.) She'd had no access to food or water, so now she always packs both. She hadn't been able to call her family because her phone died, so now she carries external phone charger/battery packs with her.

Now I travel with a wheeled carry-on bag containing two fully-charged external phone batteries, protein bars and water. This is more about being prepared should my plane get grounded somewhere for hours than anything else. I doubt that I will ever need them, but it can't hurt to be prepared!

CHAPTER SEVEN
How to Beat Jetlag

How to arrive looking and feeling glam!

Jetlag is an energy vampire that may steal the first few days of your trip if you don't take steps to beat it – or at least mitigate its symptoms. Not everyone gets it, but it's no fun if you do. I have been traveling internationally all of my adult life. In the early years, I used to get knocked sideways by jetlag, and would have days of misery at the beginning of a trip while I desperately tried to get acclimatized to the new time zone. Later, I decided that I'd worked too hard and made too many sacrifices to be able to travel and I refused to lose any days of it to this mystery ailment. So, I learned everything I could about jetlag and figured out how to control it as much as humanly possible.

What are Jetlag & Travel Fatigue?

Jetlag, or desynchronosis, is a condition caused by alterations to the body's circadian rhythms as a result of jetting at high speed across long distances of trans-meridian (west-east or east-west) travel. Traveling at a slower speed, such as by boat or propeller plane, doesn't cause jetlag. It's all about that speed. Traveling north-south doesn't seem to cause jetlag either, or at least doesn't have the severity. It is thought that the more time zones you cross, the more severe the effects of jetlag, but it really depends on the individual.

The symptoms of jetlag vary and can affect you differently from trip to trip.

The most well-known symptom is sleep disruption. Jetlag can have you wide awake all night long, or asleep on your feet during the day. Other symptoms include poor cognitive function, nausea, headaches, dizziness and digestive problems.

Another travel ailment which can occur independently of (or parallel to) jetlag is **travel fatigue**. Travel fatigue leaves you exhausted, disoriented, with headaches, and is caused by the combination of your sleep routine being disrupted, the time spent in a cramped seat with little opportunity to move around, the low oxygen environment of the plane, limited food and drink during the flight, possibly poor-quality food on the plane, dehydration and dry air. (Fortunately, travel fatigue usually only takes one day and a good night's sleep to fix itself.) I package jetlag and travel fatigue in the same box, as they make you feel equally awful, and by using the same tricks and techniques you can minimize or avoid both.

If you have traveled around the world before, you probably already know that flying from the US to Europe isn't too arduous, but any trans-Asian or Australasian travel can be brutal.

Personally, I find the flight from Los Angeles to Auckland or Sydney to be pretty easy. The flight leaves America at night, and even if I can't sleep deeply I can normally catch a nap or two. The flight arrives in the morning, local time, so your body tricks itself into not noticing the change in time zone. The adjustment is pretty painless. I might go to bed early the first night but after that I am fine. The return trip however is murder! I will have a week of waking up at 2am and not getting back to sleep, of being mind-bendingly exhausted in the middle of the day and feeling like my entire world has been tipped upside down.

If you are traveling **to Italy from Australia or New Zealand**, I sincerely recommend breaking up your trip, and also arriving in Italy a day early so that you can sleep off some of the craziness.

If you are flying **from Asia**, your flight will probably be around fourteen hours, so I also recommend arriving a day early to give you a chance to adjust and not be overtired the first day of your trip.

If flying **from the US**, you need to factor in your domestic travel to your departure city, then the length of your international flight. Most direct flights from the US to Italy arrive in the morning, local time, which makes it easier for your body to adjust to the new time zone.

How to Beat It

1. GIVE YOURSELF TIME TO RECOVER

The first step to mitigating jetlag and travel fatigue (from this point just referred to as jetlag) is in the planning of your trip. Consider what time you have to wake up and leave home to get to your first flight, then start filling in the blanks that make up your flight connections and layovers – you may save a couple of hundred dollars by choosing a flight plan with long layovers or multiple connections, but at what cost? Alternatively, if you are traveling on a really tight budget (as I have done many, many times) and you really do need to save that $200, look at arriving a day early and staying in a cheap hotel for a night. That way you can sleep off the worst of it.

2. PREPARATION

The second step in warding off jetlag is by preparing your body in the lead up to your trip.

Get extra sleep.

In the week prior to flying (two weeks if you can manage it) try to get extra sleep. Go to bed an hour earlier each night, or whatever increment of an hour you can manage, and start banking some extra sleep. A well-rested body can fight off more ailments than a tired one can!

Increase your daily exercise.

This can be by adding long walks into your day, pushing yourself to get to the gym or to yoga class, forcing yourself to go for a run – whatever your favorite form of exercise is. I am especially vigilant the day before travel and, when my flights allow, even on the day of travel. Make an effort to get the blood pumping through your veins. You will feel the difference when it counts!

Be careful with your diet.

In the week leading up to your flight cut the unhealthy things out of your diet. You already know what they are – the culprits include salty and high sodium food, processed food, sodas, sugary food and alcohol. There are some healthy foods to avoid too, including cruciferous vegetables (broccoli, brussels sprouts, cabbage, coleslaws etc). Although healthy to eat, these are likely to bloat you and make you gassy, which is uncomfortable for you and hellish for the people sitting around you on the plane!

Make sure to eat plenty of fresh, healthy food instead this week. Salads and meals with a high vegetable content paired with lean proteins are your best friends prior to long flights. They give your body the ammunition it needs to do some good fighting for you and will minimize discomfort during and after the flight.

Drink plenty of water.

In the week leading up to your flight, the day of your flight, throughout your flight and after you land, you need to chug down as much water as you can (one glass of water per hour would be ideal). One of the biggest culprits in making you feel jetlagged is dehydration. Believe it or not, your body loses the equivalent of a glass of water for each hour you spend in the air. This loss of water impacts every cell in your body. You see it in your skin and your hair, you feel it in your muscles and your overall sense of wellbeing. The loss of water can make you feel groggy, unfocused, exhausted, dizzy, and generally out-of-sorts with yourself. Lots of people get headaches after long flights due to dehydration (personally I think almost all headaches during and after flying are tied to dehydration) and if you are a migraine-sufferer like me, dehydration can trigger a chain of debilitating migraines, which would have a devastating effect on your vacation.

Take your vitamins.

In the week or two leading up to your flight, mega dose your vitamins. Vitamin C is your best, best friend when traveling, it gives your body so much ammunition to fight off all the germs you come into contact with on your flights, plus it is your body's ultimate fighting friend. I drink lots of Emergen-C prior to every trip. B vitamins, magnesium, selenium and zinc are also fantastic for travelers, both prior to departure and during travel.

Whenever I can, I get a Super Immune IV the week before I leave. (Google *Myers Cocktail Vitamins* to find a naturopath or natural wellness center near you that does Myers and Super Immune Support IVs.) These are vitamin mixes that bypass your digestive system and go into your body intravenously. The Super Immune IV (my favorite) has large doses of Vitamin C, B vitamins, plus zinc, selenium, magnesium and some other essential minerals. They make you feel fantastic, and I have noticed that I never get sick when I get an IV prior to traveling. (The only times I have been sick while traveling were the trips when I haven't had time to get across town for an IV.)

3. TRAVEL DAY

The third step to avoiding jetlag is what you do on the day you travel, and then during your flight.

Be fastidious about what you eat and drink the day you fly.

Although airports seem to be starting to get the message and are providing some healthier options now, the bulk of food on offer is still food you shouldn't eat prior to a long flight. One way around this is to bring food with you. I always travel with sliced apples, fresh raw nuts, healthy protein bars, whatever healthy food I can prepare at home that won't take up too much space in my carry-on bag. It needs to be easy to move around with (i.e it won't leak in my bag), easily eaten finger food, and doesn't require heating. I also have an empty water bottle that I fill at a water station in the gate area.

Avoid caffeine and alcohol.

I don't drink coffee prior to a long trip, as I want to be able to sleep if at all possible. Ideally, avoid alcohol pre-flight and during your flight. I will sometimes have a glass of wine with my meal on the international flight, but never more than one. Avoiding alcohol altogether is your best bet, as it will only further dehydrate you.

Wear compression socks.

Before you board your flight, put on your compression socks or hose. They are an absolute lifesaver (literally). Compression-wear will keep forcing blood back up from your feet, ankles and lower legs, preventing them from swelling. They help prevent the dreaded DVT (deep vein thrombosis), and quite honestly, after having flown with and without them I can tell you that you will feel very much better if you wear them. Note – I don't advise trying to put them on in the plane because they can be *really tricky* to put on. Unless you are in Cirque du Soleil, you may have trouble contorting sufficiently to get them on in your seat!

Adopt Italy time.

Once you are on your plane and buckled in, change your watch to Italy time and mentally move yourself into the new time zone. If it is sleeping time in Italy, you should do your very best to try to sleep after your meal on the plane. Put on some noise-cancelling headphones or use earplugs, especially if you are sitting on or behind the wing. The engine noise should become white noise, but instead it tends to be the annoying, never-ending buzz that keeps you awake throughout the flight. If you are seated in front of the wing (which pretty much means First or Business class), you don't really hear the engine noise at all.

Get some sleep.

Wrap up nice and warm, get comfortable, use an eye mask to black out any lights that are on inside the plane, and do your best to get some sleep. I use an app on my smartphone called **Sleep Pillow** that lets you create a playlist of soothing nature sounds, like rain and wind, to help you sleep. Try downloading yoga nidra and meditation guides, anything to quiet your mind and bore you to sleep. One benefit of using these types of distractions is that they can at least lull you into twilight mode, where, although you may not be properly sleeping, at least your mind is resting. I will take whatever I can get!

Some people take melatonin (doesn't work for me) or sleeping pills (also don't work for me) and have success with them. If they work for you, take them. **The worst thing you can do is to stay awake watching the inflight entertainment all night.** Even if you can't fall asleep, at least try to fake your way into a doze. You'll feel like hell when you arrive in Italy if you have stayed awake all night.

Luckily, the direct flights from the US all depart late afternoon, around 5–6pm, so it isn't hard to at least *fake* some sleep. The return flights are always day flights and I am always wide awake the entire flight, but I don't care about jetlag on the way home!

4. WHEN YOU LAND

The fourth step to minimizing jetlag is what you do when you land. The most important thing is to get yourself on Italy's schedule. If you didn't sleep on the plane, chances are you will start feeling sluggish sometime after landing, and all you'll want to do is have a nap. DON'T DO IT!!! Get to your hotel or vacation rental, have a shower, get dressed, take an Emergen-C or two and then move on with your day. The quickest and easiest way to avoid or at least minimize jetlag is to function according to the new time zone. If you succumb to napping or sleeping during daylight hours, you are confirming to your body that you are still in your home time zone. You are always better off staying awake if you can possibly manage it.

The most difficult jetlag situation is the one when you arrive at night, but your body says it's daytime and won't let you sleep. It is hell on your body and your mind. Your brain is buzzing, your limbs feel heavy, you lie down but feel like you are spinning. If that happens to you, your best bet is to take a sleep aid and try to get an artificial sleep. If nothing else, it will help reset your body clock.

My two best remedies for jetlag are to drink copious amounts of water, and to get into the sunlight. Jetlag has a lot to do with the disruption of your circadian rhythms, so you need to get outdoors into Italian daylight. It is a really easy fix on a sunny day, a little less so on a cloudy or rainy day, but regardless of the weather, go outside and walk.

I make sure I walk for at least two hours during my first day, which is easy to do in Italy because everywhere you look there are amazing things to see! Just walk and walk and walk. Walking gets your blood pumping and helps move the fluids that have been pooling in your legs, feet and ankles. If you can, stay outdoors for as long as it is light and don't go to bed until it is getting dark. Your body will more quickly adjust to the new time zone and you will feel so much better for it.

As much as you want to dive head first into a bowl of pasta, don't do it. Eat a light meal, don't have (much) alcohol and don't have coffee late in the day. I always get my first Italian coffee in the airport when I land – to me it is the best coffee in the world! But I avoid having a glass of wine that first day.

If you still don't feel right the next day, do the same thing again. Take vitamins, drink lots of water and get outside in the sun. The more you push your body into adjusting to the new time zone, the more quickly it will adapt. The more you take naps and stay in bed, the longer the adjustment will take. If you are flying from the US, jetlag isn't too big of an issue. If you are coming from Asia or Australasia it can be much harder. Just hang in there and you will be fine!

Now That You're in Italy…

Getting Around

CHAPTER EIGHT
Renting Cars

Fun or terrifying?

I absolutely love driving around Italy. Having said that, you couldn't pay me enough to drive inside Rome, Naples, Palermo or even Florence (although Florence really isn't that bad), but over the years I have driven the length and breadth of Italy as well as much of Sicily. I usually rent a stick shift/ manual transmission because they are fun to drive through the hills and on the coast roads. At home (in Phoenix) I wouldn't enjoy driving a stick, but in Italy it is a blast.

To Drive or Not to Drive?

Before I sell you on the idea of renting a car and exploring the countryside, I want you to stop and **think about whether driving would be fun for you or whether it would be a stressful nightmare.** And be honest. Some people are fine with driving in a foreign country and find it great fun and entirely liberating. For others, it can create the type of stress that ruins a trip. Don't worry! If you belong to the latter group, you will go to places you can access by train (which is a fabulous way to get around), or you can hire a driver for a day if you want to get to some of the harder-to-reach places. You will still have a wonderful time.

For those of you who are up for a drive, read on for some stories and tips about driving through Italy!

MY FIRST TIME

The idea of renting a car in Italy would never have entered my head had it not been for one of my best friends. She had rented cars and driven all over Europe with her two young children in the back seat and she was both fearless and experienced. So, when we decided to take our first trip to Italy together, she went ahead and booked a rental car. It never occurred to me that I would be expected to drive.

On the first day of our trip we were tearing through the hills of the Chianti in our little Fiat Panda, having the time of our lives with the radio blasting and me happily riding shotgun, when her husband called. She pulled over to the side of the road so that she could talk to him, then jumped out of the car and told me to drive while she was on the phone. I admit, I felt mildly nauseous, not having driven a stick shift since I was 20 and scared I was going to bunny-hop the car along the road. (I didn't – it turns out the whole stick shift thing is just like riding a bike. You don't forget how to do it.) I felt mildly terrified at the thought of driving in Italy, but I had to save face, so I got behind the wheel and off we went.

I didn't expect that driving around Italy with Michelle would be some of the most fun I have ever had. It was just so easy! Whoever was in the passenger seat would navigate and we got lost a thousand times, but in doing so we found the coolest little towns by accident. It was fantastic!

MY SECOND TIME

The following year we did it again, but this time Michelle left Italy a few days before I did, and thinking I had this driving thing down, I happily dropped her at the airport and then headed back to San Gimignano.

And everything went wrong.

I drove into the wrong lane at the toll booth and a huge line of traffic backed up behind me while I had a minor panic attack about not knowing what to do. (A motorcyclist came to my rescue and used his Telepass to make the gate open for me.)

The GPS on my smartphone couldn't quite keep up, so I kept missing exits on the motorway. Without Michelle there to navigate, I got horribly lost. My maiden solo driving voyage deposited me alone in a parking lot, on the verge of tears, wondering what on earth I had gotten myself into. Fortunately, I rallied. I decided that I had sacrificed too much to be in Italy, I still had many plans for the rest of my trip, and therefore I was going to have to find a way to make it fun. In the end, I mastered it and the remainder of my time in Italy, racing around in my little Fiat, was wonderful.

Since then I have often rented cars and have driven all over the country, but if that had been my first trip to Italy it would have ruined my entire vacation. I tell you this because I want you to think about it before making the commitment to driving during your trip to Italy.

Some of you who are reading this will leap into driving in Europe and will have endless fun doing it. Others will be like I was – nervous at first but just fine with a good friend sharing the driving and navigating duties, and after a while just fine on my own. But for the third group, driving might be too much for your first trip to Italy.

You came to Italy to have a wonderful time, so choose the path that makes your vacation the most fun for you.

Tips for Renting Cars in Italy

Most of the things I have learned on my Italian travels I have learned through trial and error. I did so many things the wrong way before I found the right way, and some of these mistakes involved renting cars. Here are some important lessons that I've learned.

YOU NEED AN INTERNATIONAL DRIVER'S LICENSE.

If you are a non-EU resident, to pick up your rental car you will need to show an International Driver's License or International Driving Permit. In the US, you can get an International Driving Permit at most AAA offices. They cost around US$25 if you have them take the passport style photo that is required. I get it all done there to save time.

For readers from other parts of the world, you should check with your local travel offices or google the requirements for you to get an International Driver's Permit or License.

YOU DON'T NEED A CAR IN THE CITY.

If you are staying in a larger town or city you really don't need a car. In fact, a car can be more of a liability than it's worth. Parking in a city is generally scarce and expensive, it can be hard to find your way around by car, and most big cities have great public transit options or taxi services that would be much easier.

BOOK YOUR RENTAL CAR DIRECTLY.

All the major international car rental companies are in Italy. Hertz, Avis, Budget, Sixt, and Maggiore all do business there. You need to book your rental car ahead of time, so **book your car directly through the rental car company**. If you are booking online, be sure you are dealing directly with the company and not a third-party service.

And here's why...

One time in Sicily, we arrived from the Aeolian Islands and went to pick up our rental car, only to discover two unfortunate things. The first was they were about to close for the day. Our paperwork said they were open until 6pm but that was incorrect, they closed at 1pm on Saturdays. (Luckily, we hadn't stopped for lunch on the way there!) Secondly, there were no cars. None. There were no rental cars in this town or the next, and not just from Hertz, who I had booked with, but also all the other car rental companies. I called Hertz and that's when I learned that the booking I had made online was actually through a third-party service, not Hertz itself, and as such they couldn't help me. I got the situation sorted out (see **Chapter 22 – Plan B** to find out how!), but had I been aware of the third-party alternative, I would have made sure I booked my car directly with Hertz.

DON'T PREPAY.

There is normally a cheaper option if you prepay for your rental car at the time of booking. *Don't do it.* There were several other people at Hertz that day raising hell with the boys behind the counter, because they had prepaid for their cars. Now not only was there no car, but they had already paid, so that portion of their travel budget was gone and they would have to pay again to get a car from a different vendor.

This was the only time in all my travels that there wasn't a rental car available, and I was somewhere relatively remote. Nevertheless, that experience made me realize that prepaying is not always a smart idea.

PICK UP YOUR CAR AT THE AIRPORT.

Most cities you are staying in will have rental car offices in the heart of the city. I advise *against* picking up your car (or returning it) at one of the city branches of the rental car company. Instead, pick up your car at the airport for the following reasons:

1. Firstly, driving inside an Italian city can be **confusing and stressful**, especially if you haven't driven there before. The cities contain one-way systems and ZTLs* that your GPS may not pick up on. It can be really stressful driving inside a city.

2. The second reason is that, even if you've prearranged it, **the rental car office may or may not be open and may or may not have your car there**. Once in Florence we had booked a rental car to be picked up at the office near our hotel in town, thinking we could save ourselves the 20-euro taxi fare to the airport rental office. We arrived with our suitcases to pick up our car and found that they had closed for the day – we were the only people scheduled for a pick up, so they took the day off!

Returning a rental car to an office in a city can also be a problem if you get there and they have decided to close early or leave for lunch, especially if you have a plane or train to catch. Trust me, it is much more reliable to return your car to the airport (even if you are not flying out). I always pick up and drop off my rental cars at the airport.

3. The third reason is that the **rental offices at the airport always have cars.**

4. The fourth reason is that **airports are usually on the edge of town** and have direct access to the motorway. This makes your exit so much easier!

Zona Traffico Limitato (ZTL*)
Limited Traffic Zone

A ZTL is an area where only business vehicles like taxis and delivery trucks, and people who live inside the ZTL and who have a special pass on their cars, can drive. These are typically old parts of town with tiny, narrow streets making a virtual labyrinth and it is nearly impossible to find your way around. ZTLs not only help protect the ancient buildings, but the traffic would be crazy if everyone could drive inside these ancient areas.

ZTLs are monitored by cameras. If you stray inside one, the cameras will catch you. Months later (thanks to slow-moving Italian bureaucracy) you will receive a sizeable fine attached to the credit card you booked your rental car with.

RENT A SMALL CAR.

For Americans reading this book, this may be more difficult to come to terms with, but you seriously do not want to rent a big car or SUV in Italy. On the motorways it makes no difference, but all the towns and villages that you'll want to visit have narrow streets that are not designed for huge vehicles. You quite literally *can't* drive a big vehicle through them – it won't fit.

Parking spaces in Italy are designed for small vehicles. Spaces are narrow and close together, so unless you can find two empty parking spaces side by side you might be stuck with nowhere to park.

Also, gasoline/petrol/diesel in Italy is expensive. I have paid the American equivalent to $7 per gallon.

Trust me, it is easier and more cost-effective to rent something small.

RENT A DIESEL.

Where possible, I rent diesels as they get better gas mileage. European diesels are also quiet, unlike most of the diesels I see in the US.

GET SUPERCOVER INSURANCE.

You really must get full Supercover insurance. It will drastically increase the price of your rental car but is well worth it in the event of anything going wrong. Supercover gives you 100% coverage, so if anything at all happens, from someone denting your door in a parking lot to a car crash, you won't have to pay so much as a dollar.

Every time I have rented a car in Italy I have been told that without Supercover there is a 3000-euro deductible should anything happen. I once read on TripAdvisor about a couple who had their passports held by the rental company until they paid the deductible. It is not worth the risk! Get the Supercover insurance.

Why you might need it...

Several years ago, while driving the Amalfi Coast with my best friend, another tourist took a bend too fast and too wide and hit us. We weren't hurt but the car was. The guy that hit us was a particularly aggressive Israeli dude who, two minutes into the info exchange, grabbed his passport back, jumped in his car and took off. Had we not purchased the Supercover insurance we would have had to come up with an additional 3000 euros, even though it was a hit and run situation.

I seldom see accidents on the roads in Italy, unlike Phoenix where I see multiple accidents every day. (This blows my mind because if you have ever been to Phoenix you will know that our freeways are generally dead straight, the lanes are wide, and the freeways are kept in fantastic condition, with no potholes. There is no reason to have car crashes here!) Regardless of there being fewer accidents in Italy, in my opinion your best bet is to get the maximum insurance.

NOTE: For my American readers, you cannot use your American car insurance the way you can when renting a car in the US.

APPOINT A NAVIGATOR.

If possible, have someone in the passenger seat reading the GPS on your phone. The road signs in Italy can be tricky to spot and if you are not sure where you are going it could be a little stressful. **I don't recommend the Google Maps app on your phone.** It is invariably incorrect in Italy. For iPhone users, Siri is right most of the time. I have another tour guide friend who swears by **WAZE** in Italy, so this year I will give that a try.

Don't trust the GPS that comes with the car. I recently had the rental car people at the airport in Florence set up the onboard GPS for me. I was driving to San Gimignano, a drive I have done many, many times so I know it well, but I wanted to see how the GPS system worked. It kept getting everything completely wrong! As in *crazy wrong*. I would have been hopelessly lost if I was relying on it to get me anywhere.

If you will be relying on WiFi while you are away, there are smartphone apps that will give you directions offline.

READ AHEAD.

Whoever is navigating needs to be watching the next instruction rather than waiting for the GPS to tell you aloud. I have often found that whichever map/GPS service I am using, it can't quite keep up, so you may be well past a turn or past the ability to get into the turning lane by the time the voice tells you. I prefer to know that I will be turning right in 500 meters than waiting for the GPS to tell me to turn right.

PRINT MAPS AHEAD OF TIME.

When I am going to be driving somewhere new I like to google it before I leave so I have an idea of where I am going. I look at the step-by-step version so that I know which motorways I will be getting on and which exits to look for.

If I am extra-organized I will print out the directions ahead of time. If you get into a situation where your smartphone GPS keeps rerouting or sending you in circles you will be glad to have the printed directions to guide you.

NEVER LEAVE ANYTHING IN THE CAR.

Keep all belongings locked in the trunk of the rental car when it is parked. Even hats and sweatshirts and things you may think wouldn't be appealing to thieves. Obviously, phones, handbags, and shopping bags need to be kept out of sight, but also children's video games, spare shoes, jackets – basically everything needs to be locked in the trunk!

Most of Europe has issues with gypsies, and plenty of countries have high unemployment. Realistically, someone desperate, who has nothing, may be more likely to break into a car to get something as simple as a sweater to keep them warm.

UNDERSTAND THE SYSTEM

Italians drive on the right-hand side of the road. When you drive on Italian motorways, you will see that they generally have two lanes in each direction. The right lane is for driving, the left lane for passing. Unless you are passing someone, **stay in the right lane**.

WATCH FOR SPEED TRAPS

There are video speed traps on the motorways. Keep pace with the other cars but be careful about speeding. If a camera catches you, it may take more than a year for the fine to reach you but reach you it will! And the fines can be *really expensive*. By the time it reaches you, there will be a fee from the rental car company, plus the fine, plus penalties for not paying in inside 60 days. It can add up quickly and will be traced back to the credit card of the person who booked the car.

Parking fines will find their way back to you too, so make sure you park only where you are allowed and leave your parking-paid slip clearly visible on the dashboard.

CHAPTER NINE
How to Use the Train System

The best way to see Italy

If you are hustling through a train station and don't have time to read this chapter in long form, jump ahead to the end, where there's a step-by-step guide to buying tickets and navigating a station.

Your Options

In my opinion the very best way to travel around Italy is by train. Italy has an amazing rail network. It runs like clockwork, connecting all the major cities as well as the smaller cities and most small towns. The high-speed trains that connect the big cities make the entire country accessible to you. You can easily buzz around the country and take day trips to cities you may otherwise have missed visiting or that would take *hours* to drive to.

Not only are the trains incredibly efficient *and* inexpensive, they are also a lovely way to travel. The seating is surprisingly comfortable, so you can sit back and enjoy the majesty of this gorgeous country through the huge, panoramic windows.

FOR EXAMPLE...

If you are staying in Rome but would love to see Venice, you can take a high-speed train and be there in less than four hours. If you are staying in Florence but have always wanted to visit Capri – no problem! You can take the high-speed train to Naples and then the ferry or hydrofoil to Capri, giving yourself a wickedly glamorous day trip!

HIGH-SPEED

The **high-speed** routes are serviced by two companies:

- **Trenitalia** high-speed trains are called AV or Alta Velocita. They are divided into three categories: Frecciarossa (Red Arrow), Frecciargente (Silver Arrow) and Frecciabianco (White Arrow), each servicing different routes, with FrecciaRossa being the fastest. Frecciarossa trains reach up to 190 MPH/300KMH.

- Ferrari-owned **Italo** has sleek, streamlined trains, which reach speeds of up to 220MPH/360KMH.

INTERCITY

Intercity trains connect major cities to smaller cities. They are not as fast as the high-speed trains, cover medium to long distances, make more stops, and connect 200 stations across Italy each day.

REGIONAL

Regional trains are smaller and slower and stop at every station. They are very inexpensive and are ideal for shorter journeys.

Buying Train Tickets

EURAIL PASSES

You can use your Eurail pass on the high-speed trains, but you have to pay an extra fee including a fee for reservation, which is mandatory. I have found that if you are traveling just within Italy you can do it less expensively without a Eurail pass.

BUYING TICKETS ONLINE

If you are able to plan your travel ahead of time (before arriving in Italy) I recommend buying your **high-speed train tickets** online. Buy them as early as possible, because the price creeps up as you get closer to the travel date.

I buy my tickets online either directly through the **Trenitalia** or **Italo** websites, or through **Rail Europe**. Trenitalia and Italo websites are in Italian but have the option to change languages. (For my American readers, click on the symbol of the British flag to translate the website into English.) The Rail Europe website is already in English and covers both high-speed train companies, but it has an additional US$7 administration fee per ticket.

The trains offer several classes of travel, from Executive to First class to Second class, with tickets priced accordingly. If you are shopping for tickets online, you can frequently find great deals on First class seats, costing only a couple of dollars more than Second class seats, or oddly enough sometimes even costing less! One time on a six-hour train ride from Milan to Salerno, I bought Executive class seats for substantially less than First class, and we rode all six hours with in-seat dining service (as many drinks and snacks as we wanted) included in the price, and seats that fully reclined. It was fantastic!

If you've purchased your tickets online, just print out your boarding pass and board your train, there is no validation required. You can also carry your boarding pass on your smartphone.

Buying Tickets at the Train Station

The other two ways to buy your ticket are at a **train station ticket counter** (where the staff will issue your ticket) or at a **self-serve kiosk**.

The **self-serve kiosk** is easy to use. **Italo kiosks are separate from Trenitalia kiosks**. Select your language and follow the prompts. If you get stuck or need help, ask a representative from the train company you are buying from (Trenitalia or Italo). They are always in uniform. It's probably better not to accept help from people hanging around the kiosk as they may be pickpockets or con artists looking to separate tourists from their money. (Having said that, I learned how to use the trains and the ticket kiosks from random strangers helping me and have always found Italians to be very kind and friendly. I *was* somewhat selective about who I would ask, however.)

Locating Your Platform (Binario)

Once you have your ticket in hand you need to figure out which platform or *binario* your train will be departing from. Your ticket will have the train number on it; for the high-speed trains this will be a four-digit number; for the regional trains there may be more digits.

CHECK THE DEPARTURE (*PARTENZA*) BOARD FOR...

Once you know your train number, you need to find it on the departure board. There will be two boards, **Arrivi** for arriving trains and **Partenza** for departing trains. You want the **Partenza** board. Look for your train number, which will be in the left-hand column. Next to that column, the final stop for your train will be listed.

...YOUR DESTINATION.

Imagine you're in Naples and wanting to travel to Florence. The train's final stop isn't Florence, it is Milan, so next to the train number it will say *Milano*. Remember *everything will be in Italian*. Some of the departure boards scroll through the stops the train will make along the route. In this scenario, your train will stop at Roma Tiburtina (Rome, Tiburtina station), Roma Termini (Rome, Termini station), Firenze Rifredi (Florence, Rifredi station), Firenze S.M.N (Florence Santa Maria Novella – the station you are getting off at), Bologna and finally Milano Cle. If you were looking for the word 'Florence', you wouldn't see it!

... YOUR PLATFORM.

The *partenza* board will announce your platform 10–15 minutes prior to departure. The platform numbers are easily spotted at the front of each platform. Look across them and notice which direction the numbering goes, and which number platforms are in front of you to figure out which direction to move in once your platform is announced.

Depending on which station you're at, there will be agents checking tickets either between the concourse and the platforms, or on the platform itself.

If they are between the concourse and the platforms, I like to move through ahead of time and watch the *partenza* board from the other side. It speeds things up when the platform is actually announced.

Validate Your Ticket

If you purchased your ticket at the station (from a kiosk or the ticket counter), you will need to validate it. There are validation machines at the beginning of each platform (as well as along the platform). Use the time spent waiting for your platform to be announced to locate a validation machine, insert your ticket, and have it validated. **You MUST validate your ticket.**

Your Seat Assignment

If you are taking a high-speed train your seat assignment will be printed on your ticket. Look for the word ***Carrozza***, which means *carriage*. Next to or below it will be a number. This is your train carriage number. Let's say your ticket says *Carrozza 9*. Next it will have your seat number. It may say ***Finestrino*** for window seat or ***Corridoio*** for aisle seat.

Imagine that the *partenza* board has announced your train platform will be Number 16. Go to Platform 16, and as you walk along the platform, look up at the small screens overhead that indicate which train carriage will be stopping where. Walk to where it says *Carrozza 9*. As your train pulls in you will see the carriages are marked with their number, and on the door, it will show seats 1–15 at one end and 15–30 at the other (or whichever numbering it has). Try to board from the end closest to your seat number.

Once Aboard

LUGGAGE

Most AV trains will have a luggage section at one end of the carriage, and it fills up quickly. The rows of seats have an open, inverted V shape between them. This is for you to slide your suitcase into if the luggage section is full. I always put my suitcase there anyway, so no one can leave the train with it without my noticing.

The train will leave the station quite quickly, so hustle on board, **leave your cabin baggage on your seat while you put your suitcase away**, then put your other bags in the overhead rack. Your train will be filling up and other passengers need to get past you. It is incredibly frustrating to be trying to reach your seat with your luggage and not be able to get past someone who is taking up the aisle whilst monkeying around with their bags, so be considerate.

Keep your ticket with you. The conductor will come by and check your ticket to make sure you are on the right train, in the right seat and have a validated ticket.

Now kick back, relax, and enjoy the view!

Train Station Guide

If you are hustling through the train station and need a fast guide, no problem. Here it is step-by-step.

1. At the ticket kiosk, **change the language** to English by pressing the British flag (the Union Jack).

2. **Follow the prompts** to enter which city you want to travel to.

3. **Pay** for your ticket.

4. Once your ticket prints out, look on your ticket for your **train number**.

5. Locate the *partenza* **board**.

6. Look for your **train number** on the left-hand side of the *partenza* board.

7. Next to the train number it will say the final stop for that train. It will hopefully scroll through the stops along the way. Remember your stop will be in **Italian not English**. Naples = Napoli, Florence = Firenze, Venice = Venezia etc.

8. **Validate your ticket** in the small validation machine at the beginning of any platform.

9. Look on your ticket for the word ***Carrozza*** and the number, to see which carriage you are in.

10. Look on your ticket for your **seat number and assignment** (***Finestrino*** for window seat or ***Corridoio*** for aisle seat).

11. Look at the platform numbers to see in which direction they go, and which platform is nearest to you.

12. Pass through the **ticket check** and get to the platform side of the concourse.

13. Watch the *partenza* board to see which platform (***binario/bin***) your train will depart from. It will be announced 10–15 minutes prior to departure.

14. Once on the train, put your **suitcases** in the space between your seat and the seat behind it. Put your other belongings in the overhead rack and take your seat as quickly as possible.

15. Keep your ticket close by for the conductor to check.

16. Look out the window and enjoy the view! Happy travels!

Eating & Drinking

CHAPTER TEN
How to Order Coffee in Italy

Experience Italy's culture

I thought about titling this chapter *A Beginner's Guide to Coffee Culture in Italy*, because coffee is really a part of the culture. Standing at the bar in a coffee shop, knocking back an espresso (*un caffè*) is part of the social fabric in this very social country, and if you get the system and your order down, you'll feel like a local in no time.

Embrace the Differences

The first thing to know is that coffee in Italy is nothing like Starbucks.

Drinks generally come in one size and are intended to be consumed onsite. Stomping your foot and demanding a venti will get you exactly nowhere (venti means *twenty* in Italian, so who knows what you might be served!). Your drink will be served in a real cup, not a paper cup. Italians don't walk around eating and drinking in the streets as we do in the US. It's different and (in my opinion) it's even better.

Learn the System

The second thing to know is that there is a system you need to learn and follow.

When you walk into a *café* (coffee bar) assess the situation before walking up to the bar. In most big city establishments you will need to pay the cashier first. He will give you a receipt to take up to the bar to place your order. In smaller coffee shops you can order and pay at the bar.

If you are going to eat something – a pastry, a biscotto, a sandwich etc, you need to scope out what's behind the glass before you pay for your order. Have a look, decide what you want and then go tell the cashier. Normally everything in a given food category costs the same. Panini are one price, all the pastries are one price etc, but there can be variables, so it doesn't hurt to check first.

Now with your receipt in hand, go up to the bar and get the barista's attention. He or she will grab your receipt, ask you what you're having, and then tear it so they know the order has been filled.

There will be two prices for the coffee you are ordering. One is for drinking it standing at the bar and the other is for taking it to sit at a table. It is cheaper to drink it standing at the bar. (Italians drink their coffee at the bar.)

It should be noted at this point that a coffee in Italy (*un caffè*) is what we would call *a shot of espresso* in the US.

Ordering

There is no equivalent in Italy to American drip coffee and you won't find Coffeemate or flavored coffee creamers. Italian coffee ruins you – it is so incredibly good. After a vacation in Italy, it is near impossible to go back to drinking Starbucks!

HOW TO ORDER

The way to ask for your order is to say, *Un caffe per favore*.

In a busy joint you can get away with just saying the name of the drink you want, but you probably will have to get the barista's attention. To do that you can say, *Scusi,* or just make eye contact.

WHAT TO ORDER

Un Caffe

Un caffe is a shot of espresso. It will be served to you in a little cup on a saucer with a teaspoon for sugar. Usually you will also be given a small glass of water on the side.

Un Macchiato or Un Macchiato Caldo

This is nothing like the huge sugary confection served stateside. It's a shot of espresso *stained* (made *macchiato*) with a drop of milk. If you want the milk to be hot and foamed ask for *Macchiato Caldo*. It is still served in a little espresso cup.

Un Caffe Con Panna

This is similar to a macchiato but is sweeter, and instead of milk is topped with a dollop of whipped cream.

Un Cappuccino or Cappuccio

This is served in a bigger cup, but still is not as large as the American tall drink. A cappuccino is a shot of espresso with foamed milk. Italians only drink this from breakfast time until mid-morning. (My Italian friends cringe at the thought of milk sitting on a full stomach.) However, being that you probably are not his first tourist, your barista will happily make you cappuccinos all day long.

Un Americano

This is the closest thing you will get to an American drip coffee. Sort of. It's a shot of espresso with hot water added. Chances are it will still be much stronger than the coffee you are used to. Also, this drink is strictly for the tourists – no Italian would be caught dead drinking it.

Un Caffe Lungo

You can ask for a *caffe lungo* (long) for a slightly weaker version of a standard *caffe*.

Un Corretto or *Caffe Corretto*

This is "corrected" coffee, being "corrected" with a shot of liquor! It could be grappa, brandy, Sambuca, Cognac or I'm sure anything you would prefer.

Italians pop into a café/ bar multiple times per day. It's a fun habit to take part in. If espresso seems too strong to start with just load it up with sugar. You will get the hang of it and develop a taste for it in no time. Before you know it you'll be drinking it straight or with just a little sugar.

CHAPTER ELEVEN
How to Make Coffee in a Moka Pot

When in Rome...

If you are staying in a vacation rental villa, apartment or agriturismo, or if your hotel room has a kitchen, you probably won't find an American-style drip coffee maker but instead will find an Italian coffee pot called a *moka*.

Mokas are easily identifiable as most of them are eight-sided, and you are not likely to find any other octagonal objects in the kitchen!

As I've mentioned, Italians don't drink long (big) cups of coffee like we do. Mokas are used to make stovetop espresso – short shots of strong, espresso coffee. If you need a long cup, like you have at home, you can create an Americano coffee by adding boiling water to the espresso in your cup. It is stronger than drip coffee but it will give you a larger cup of morning brew.

The first time I came across a moka I had no idea how to use it, or what it was called, so I couldn't even google how to use it. (This was prior to my learning to speak Italian.) The housekeeper for the apartment I was renting spoke zero English, but she came over to demonstrate how the gizmo worked.

When you get the hang of using a moka you will love it!

Step-by-step

A moka has three parts. There is the **base**, inside which sits a **funnel-shaped piece** with a perforated cup, and then there is the **jug** portion, which screws on to the top of the base and has a lid and a handle.

1. Start by unscrewing the jug portion from the base. Fill the base with water, leaving a centimeter gap at the top.

2. Now sit the funnel inside the opening of the base. Once you have it in place, fill the perforated cup with ground coffee.

3. Then screw the jug portion back onto the base.

4. Now put the moka on the stove over a flame that is no wider than the base of the moka. (If it is wider you will heat up the handle.)

5. A moka works like a percolator. The water in the base heats up and pushes up through funnel basket, through the ground coffee in the perforated cup, and into the jug portion of the moka, where it is collected for you to drink. It takes a few minutes to heat up, but you can lift the lid to check the progress.

6. **When the top portion is filled with coffee it is ready!**

Note: Before you grab the handle of the moka, check that it hasn't heated up, as it could burn you. I normally use a kitchen towel or cloth to pick up the moka, having burned myself on a hot handle more than once!

Ground Coffee

My favorite ground coffee to buy in Italy is Illy or Lavazza Crema e Gusto. I usually buy several bricks of Lavazza to carry back to use in my moka at home in the US, although you can also buy it on Amazon.

Note: If you use flavored creamers in your coffee at home, you may want to pack some with you as you won't find them in Italy.

Still confused?

You'll find a pictorial guide on **How to Make Italian Coffee with a Moka** on my blog. https://corinnabsworld.com/2017/09/how-to-make-italian-coffee-moka.html

CHAPTER TWELVE
Drinking Wine in Italy

Salute!

I wonder how many travelers look forward to drinking wine while they are in Italy? Personally, I am always looking forward to my next glass of Italian wine!

Italy has a rich history of wine, dating back more than 2000 years (possibly more than 3000 years). The Etruscans, who were running the show from 800 BC to 509 BC when the Romans took over, were grape traders and wine makers. They introduced wine-making grapes to the Emilia-Romagna region of Italy in the 7th century BC. Meanwhile the Greeks were introducing varieties of wine-making grapes to Italy's deep south at around the same time, 800 BC. Italy and wine are inextricably intertwined!

No Sulfites, No Hangovers

There is magic in the wine in Italy. Or maybe there is magic in the lack of sulfites in the wine in Italy. If you usually can't drink red wine because it gives you a headache, then this is your lucky day! While in Italy you will be able to drink red wine until it comes out of your ears and will still wake up headache-free. So those of you who were about to skip this chapter, thinking there would be a hangover at the end of it, stay with me and read on!

I am a migraine specialist – I have been getting migraines my entire life, and as much as I love red wine it has always been my arch enemy. To this day just one glass of California red is a guaranteed migraine either during the night or when I wake up in the morning. The only exception for me is when I am in Italy. **In Italy I can drink red wine every day, as many glasses as I want, with no migraine.**

What we call organic wine they just call wine. Locals have explained to me that there are no GMOs in Italy, no tampering with the vines. Just hearty grapes grown in good soil. At the other end of the production there are no additives either. Just wine.

One of my Glam Italia women once told me she couldn't drink wine because it always made her face hurt. She would wake up the next morning with her sinuses aching, and generally feeling like hell. I coerced her into trying wine in Italy, and not only did it not make her feel sick the next day (or any of the days on her tour), but she shipped home cases of wine from a winery we visited in Tuscany.

Order Local

In Italy, wine is regional, just like the cuisine. Ideally you should drink the wine from the region you are in. Rather than ordering a bottle of Merlot or Chardonnay as you would at home, order the *local* red or white wine. If you are in Lecce having lunch, don't order a *Chianti* or a *Brunello* (those are Tuscan wines). Instead order a *Primativo*. Don't worry if you don't know the name of a local wine. In Italy wine is part of the culture, and everyone will know their local wines, including your waiter.

Although I travel around all over Italy and I know my favorite wines in my favorite places, I am far from fluent in wines nationwide (See **Chapter 13 – Regional Wine Guide** for a list). So, when I'm dining somewhere new in Italy, I always tell my waiter that I want a local wine from that town, or the immediate area. It gives him a chance to tell me the story of his local wines and pair something perfect for what we are eating.

Wine grown in a given area is the best compliment to ingredients grown, caught and harvested in that area, and consuming local wine is a fabulous way to learn about the place you are visiting.

Co-op Wine

I always like eating at little local restaurants, rather than big chic places that you have to get dressed up for. In many of the smaller towns, the local pizza place, or the little restaurant in town will make a **co-op wine**. Everyone in the area pools their grapes at harvest time and one big local wine is made. They each get as many demijohns of wine as per the volume of grapes they contributed.

When ordering co-op wine at these restaurants, it is served at your table in a jug. It usually costs around 4 euros for the entire jug and tastes so good you won't believe it! I can't imagine finding a US$4 bottle of wine that didn't taste like paint thinner or make you violently ill, but in Italy there are fabulous wines to be found with an extremely inexpensive price tag.

Trust the Locals

On my first trip to Sicily with my mother and my son, we arrived late on a Sunday afternoon, when all the shops were closed. The little beach town we were staying in had a mini mart that was still open, so we stopped in there to pick up some food and drink supplies.

I knew nothing about Sicilian wine, so I asked the woman behind the counter if she could advise me. She walked me along her wine wall, explaining the different wines until she reached the end where a handful of dusty, label-free bottles were sitting to the side. "These," she said, "are *my* wines. I made them myself!" They cost 5 euros (US$5-ish) per bottle. I knew there was no way I could leave without a bottle and not hurt her feelings.

In the split second it took me to hesitate, she whipped out a photo album and showed me photos of her vines, her grapes, herself with her vines, herself holding bunches of clipped grapes, and her entire wine-making process. She was incredibly proud of her wine. My heart sank. Pre-photo album, I could have bought a bottle of her wine and another bottle of something else. Post-photo album, me buying a different wine would imply that I didn't have faith in her wine-making ability.

It had been a really long travel day, I'd got lost trying to find the apartment and had driven several hair-raising loops around the one-way system in this little town. I was frazzled and just wanted to sit on my balcony with a glass of wine and look at the ocean. I had been hoping for a really good glass of wine. Oh well. With some fresh bread, prosciutto, fruit, cheeses and a bottle of her wine, we headed back to our beautiful rental apartment.

Up until that point I had little to no experience with $5 bottles of wine and I was sure it would taste like turpentine and make us sick. Still, after looking at the bottle for a while I decided to open it anyway. We could just try a sip.

I have to tell you, it was one of the loveliest wines I have ever had anywhere in the world! Sicilian wines have a fabulous peppery note to them, the vines having grown in mineral rich, volcanic soil. The woman's wine had the peppery finish but was infused with the mellow notes of the fruit trees that I had seen in her photos, bordering her little patch of vines. We couldn't believe that anything so beautiful could, firstly, only cost 5 euros and, secondly, be made by the woman who owns the mini mart!

The next morning, I went back to the mini mart to buy more, scared that some other traveler would get ahead of me and buy them all. I decided to go back every day to get another bottle. The joy on her face and the opportunity to hear another handful of stories made it an experience I didn't want to miss by buying several bottles at once! Over the course of the week, she introduced me to all of her family members, and she and I became fast friends!

It was a valuable lesson.

A couple of years later I was in Sicily again, this time traveling with my best friend. We rented an apartment on the southeast coast in a beach town called Avola, home of the famous Nero d'Avola grape, the most important red wine grape in all of Sicily. (Although I hadn't actually made that connection when I booked the apartment – I just loved the photos of this gorgeous apartment with the giant terrace overlooking the ocean.) The landlord was a wonderful fellow who owned several vacation rentals as well as a field of olive trees and another of vines. (If you stay at one of his properties during harvest time, he lets you join in and take part in the making of olive oil and/or wine.)

We were there a month before the harvest, so missed the action, but the landlord did bring us a bottle of his wine when we arrived. This time I was prepared, and while my bestie looked a little horrified at the dusty, home-corked, label-free bottle, I knew there would be magic inside. And there was! His wine was so sensational you didn't want to speak. We sat out on the giant terrace with the view of the ocean, inhaling the aroma of his wine and savoring each exquisite sip.

The point I'm trying to make is that you need to throw yourself wholeheartedly into trying the simplest of local wines and not get too caught up in brands and vintages and appellations. Italy has amazing wines at every level and every price point. If you are traveling and have the money to buy expensive Italian wines, they are fabulous, and you will love them. But do try the simple wines too, because they can be magical.

CHAPTER THIRTEEN
Italian Wines by Region

In vino veritas

As I've said, wherever you are in Italy, ideally drink the wine of that region. Rather than ordering a Chianti because you want a glass of red wine, ask for one of the well-known reds from the area you are in. The same goes with whites, sparkling wines and rosés.

Italy offers incredible diversity in wine styles and in grape varieties. The country is divided into twenty administrative regions (similar to states), and each of these regions has its own wine regions within, each with its own wine specialties and its own wine style. Some regions are known for their volume (Puglia, Veneto) and others for their exclusive grape varieties, (such as Tuscany's Brunello, a wine exclusive to a 3000-acre area around Montalcino).

Italian wines are classified by a four-tier appellation hierarchy. Every wine-producing country has to have laws in place to separate the cost-effective bulk wines from the best and most exclusive wines. These laws ensure that only the grapes specific to that particular wine are used and that the wine isn't padded out with a cheaper grape.

The Four Wine Appellations

1. Denominazione di Origine Controllata e Garantita (DOCG)

The DOCG appellation is reserved for the very highest quality wines from Italy. The wine must meet the legal requirements for DOC wines as well as pass a blind taste test. There are additional limitations including alcohol content and permitted yield from the vines and the winery – there are even laws against irrigating the vines! During droughts, DOCG vines need approval to be given water. The rules are incredibly stringent in order to keep this prestigious classification for only the very best wines from Italy.

2. Denominazione di Origine Controllata (DOC)

The DOC label was created in 1963 to protect the international reputation of Italian wines by forcing wine-makers to focus on quality. There are very strict guidelines for the production of a DOC wine, ensuring only the permitted grape varieties are used and that the wine meets all legal requirements to have the designation from the area it represents.

3. Indicazione Geografica Tipica (IGT)

This appellation was introduced in 1992 in order to separate wines that don't qualify for DOC status but are superior to basic table wines. Some of the newer "Super Tuscan" wines are made from non-Italian grapes, so don't qualify for DOC, but still need some form of status recognition. This has allowed wine-makers to experiment with grapes not native to their own region, and to create new wines and blends that are still superior in quality.

4. Vino da Tavola

This is table wine, the most basic of Italian wines. It is normally a mass-produced wine created for local consumption and doesn't require or isn't suitable for aging. Wine makers can use any grapes, the only stipulation is that the wine must be produced in Italy. These bulk wines can be shipped in large vats to other countries for bottling.

Wines to Try (By Region)

The following is a beginner's guide of wines to try in each of the twenty administrative regions of Italy. There are many different wines in each region, and most regions have wines falling into each of the four appellations. Some wines made this list because they are my personal favorites, others because my sommelier friends or Italian friends from the area insisted they be included. I haven't been to every region, and I haven't tried every wine, but this is the list I refer to when I am traveling around Italy.

ABRUZZO	**Reds**	**Whites**
	Montepulciano d' Abruzzo	Trebbiano d' Abruzzo
	Cerasuolo Montepulciano d' Abruzzo	
AOSTA VALLEY	**Reds**	**Whites**
	Syrah Valle d'Aosta	Blanc de Morgex et de la Salle
	Valle d'Aosta Pinot Gris	
	Torrette Superieur Valle d'Aosta DOC	

BASILICATA	**Reds**	**Whites**	
	Aglianico del Vulture	Malvasia Bianca	
	Aglianico	Asprino	
	Primitivo	Vulcanella Bianco	
	Vino Spumante Rosso		
	(sparkling red)		

CALABRIA	**Reds**	**Whites**	
	Ciro	Greco di Bianco	

CAMPANIA	Reds	**Whites**	
	Aglianico	Fiano	
	Piedirosso	Falanghina	
		Greco di Tufo	

EMILIO-ROMAGNA	**Reds**	Whites	
	Gutturnio	Albana	
	Malvasia	Pignoletto	
	Barbera		
	Bonarda		
	Lambrusco		
	Sangiovese		

FRUILI VENEZIA GIULIA	**Reds**	**Whites**	**Orange**
	Pignolo	Friulano	Carso
	Schioppettino	Ramandolo	
		Ribolla	
		Gialla	
		Collio	

LAZIO	**Reds**	**Whites**	
	Cesanese	Castelli Romani	
	Super Lazio	Frascati	
	Velletri	Est! Est!! Est!!! di	
		Montefiasconi	
		Grechetto	
		Bellone	

LIGURIA	Reds	Whites
	Rossese	Cinqueterre
	Ormeasco	Pigato
		Vermentino
		Schiaccetra (sweet)

LOMBARDY	Reds	Whites
	Valtellina Nebbiolo (also	Franciacorta/Spumante
	known as Spanna)	(Champagne method)
		Oltrepo Pavese

LE MARCHE	Reds	Whites
	Rosso Conero	Verdicchio
	Rosso Piceno	Offida Pecorino
	Offida Rosso	Vernaccia di Serrapetrona
	Lacrima di Morro	Esino Bianco
	Sangiovese	

MOLISE   Biferno and Pentro di Isernia are the 2 main DOC's in Molise, each making reds, whites and rosés.

The newer Molise del Molise DOC also makes reds, whites and rosés, but has a spumante as well.

Biferno reds are a blend of Montepulciano and Aglianico and Pentro di Isernia red blend Montepulciano and Sangiovese.

PIEDMONT	Reds	Whites
	Barolo	Moscato d'Asti
	Barbaresco	Asti Spumante
	Barbera d' Asti	Gavi

PUGLIA	Reds	Whites
	Primativo	Bombino Bianco
	Negroamaro	
	Uva di Troia	

SAN MARINO	Reds	Whites	
	Brugnetto	Roncale	
	Tessano	Moscato Spumante	
	Sangiovese	Oro dei Goti	

SARDINIA/	Reds	Whites	
SARDEGNA	Cannonau	Vermentino	
	Carignano	Nuragus	
	Cagnulari	Torbato	
	Malvasia	Vernaccia	
		Semidano	

SICILY	Reds	Whites	Dessert Wines
	Nero d'Avola	Carricante	Passito di Pantelleria
	Frappato	Corinto	
	Gaglioppo	Grillo	
	Perricone	Marsala	

TRENTINO-	Reds	Whites	
ALTO ADIGE	Schiava	Pinot Grigio	
	Lagrein	Pinot Bianco	

TUSCANY	Reds	Whites	Other
	Chianti	Vernaccia di	Vin Santo
	Brunello	San	(at the end of a meal,
	Vino Nobile di	Gimignano	dip *cantucci* into a small
	Montepulciano		glass of Vin Santo)
	Bolgheri		
	Super Tuscans		

UMBRIA	Reds	Whites	
	Montefalco	Orvieto	
	Rosso di Torgiano	Bianco di Torgiano	
	Lago di Corbara		

VENETO	Reds	Whites	
	Valpolicella	Prosecco	
	Amarone	Soave	

CHAPTER FOURTEEN
How to Choose a Restaurant

Eating out in Italy can be magical.

Instead of the homogenized chain restaurants so prevalent here in the United States, almost every restaurant in Italy is owner-operated. My favorite restaurants in Italy are always little family-owned and operated places with small menus featuring recipes made from local seasonal food.

The food is always fantastic, and the service is varying degrees of wonderful and fun. The ambience is a product of gregarious, food-loving people enjoying themselves rather than a contrived environment with carefully selected décor and a playlist pre-programed to make you think you are somewhere you are not. (To keep it simple, I will refer to them all as restaurants, but be aware that there are multiple types of eateries in Italy.)

Here is a crash course in the types of eateries that you will see as you wander:

A BAR

A bar is not like a pub or a bar at home. In Italy, a bar is generally a place to go to grab a coffee and maybe a snack, such as a breakfast pastry or a sandwich. (Some bars will have alcohol as well.)

Tavola Calda

This is a bar that also serves hot food. You will see finger food like arancini as well as a variety of other hot food choices under heat lamps.

Pizzeria or Osteria

This is casual dining in a relaxed atmosphere. These are typically family-owned and family-run.

Trattoria

This is also casual dining and is usually medium-priced. These are typically family-owned and family-run.

Ristorante

These places are a little more formal, the menus tend to be a little or a lot more gourmet, and these are the priciest places to eat at.

Restaurant Culture

The first time you meet an Italian you are a stranger, the second time you meet them you are friends, and never more so than in restaurants that you revisit.

One of my favorite restaurants in Rome is **Carlo Mente, in the Trastevere**, the neighborhood where I always stay. This place is packed every night and there is always a line of local Italians waiting to be seated. I go there every single time I am in Rome, and even though they must see thousands of people in between my visits, they always remember me and welcome me by name.

Sometimes I arrive with friends or the women from my tours, but I also go there alone. Though madly busy, they always take the time to rush over when they see me in line and give me a hug and an "Ah, there you are! It's good to see you again!" even if I was only there the week before.

Because this place is so popular and the line of customers waiting to be seated can weave its way down the street, the tables are pushed together with no room for even one more chair, so they can't give me a table to myself when I'm there alone. Instead they find a table of friendly people with a spare chair and seat me there. Italians being Italians no one seems bothered that there is an interloper at their table. Instead they are always welcoming, friendly and fun, and I wind up having a blast and making a group of new friends. That to me is a perfect evening in Rome.

Another of my favorite pastimes, when I have an evening to myself in Rome, is to wander over to the Jewish Ghetto for some *carciofi* (artichokes) and a plate of pasta. I like walking into the ghetto from the Teatro Marcello/Synagogue end, because the view is so quintessentially Rome. The fabulous old pedestrian street lined with restaurants, tables lining the sidewalks in front of fantastic old buildings, Romans out and about, enjoying their evening and their magnificent city.

Fiercely loyal to any business that treats me well, I always go to the same restaurant and dine al fresco, watching the world go by. (I order the same meal each time, because it is just so incredibly good!). This restaurant is at the far end of the street, but whoever sees me first, be it a waiter or the host, will drop what they're doing, come to meet me, and escort me into the restaurant. I am told it's so that no other restaurant can steal my business, but I think it's just because Italians are flirty and fun! When I am dining alone, the waiters and maitre'd will come over and chat. When you are dining alone in Italy you are never really alone! Most of them have become my Facebook friends too, which I think is doubly charming.

From my many trips to Italy I probably have a hundred restaurant stories, but the point is I have these stories only because of the types of restaurants I choose.

Do you remember the scene in *National Lampoon's European Vacation* where the Griswolds are ordering lunch at a restaurant in Paris? They think they are ordering expensive French food, but instead the kitchen staff are just opening cans of supermarket food and bottles of cheap wine they would never drink themselves. Waiters at restaurants in popular tourist destinations see unsuspecting tourists all day every day and they may be inclined to take advantage of you.

I want you to have great dining experiences like mine, so let's look at the rules for how to choose a restaurant in Italy.

The Rules when Choosing Where to Eat

1. KEEP WALKING.

The first rule when choosing a restaurant is that no matter how hungry you are, if you are near a big monument or tourist site, or any crowded tourist area, turn your back to it and walk three or four blocks in the opposite direction.

Restaurants in densely touristy areas tend to be overpriced and serve food the locals, who are very discerning when it comes to food, would never eat. These restaurants serve quickly-prepared food to tourists who don't know any better. They know that no matter what they serve, those tables will turn over every half hour or so and their customers are unlikely to return anyway, so quality takes a back seat to profit.

Of course, there are exceptions, but remember, you have paid far too much money for this trip to be wasting your time and your taste buds on overpriced, average food. You came for the Italian experience, and the Italian experience means fantastic dining at affordable prices! If you observe the people dining in those touristy places, you will see that they are all tourists, not local Italians.

You want to eat where the Italians are eating. Keep walking.

2. USE YOUR IMAGINATION.

The second rule is don't eat anywhere with pictures on the menu. If a menu has pictures of the food, then this restaurant is designed to capture the gullible tourist market. Keep walking until you find a menu that is text-based and then use your imagination.

3. FOLLOW A LOCAL.

The third rule is look for restaurants where the locals eat. *You* should eat where the locals eat. This is your guarantee of fabulous food at a decent price. The average Italian is not going to frequent any restaurant that is overpriced or where the food is substandard. This is why you don't see them grabbing a quick lunch or dinner in a touristy eatery. Italians want beautifully prepared meals made with fresh ingredients by chefs who care about food. And they don't want to break the bank to get them. Food is a huge and important part of

Italian culture, and as a tourist in Italy you should experience the real thing.

4. FIND A PICCOLO.

Look for little restaurants on side streets. Italy is full of restaurants – they are literally everywhere. You will see them all over the busy streets, but if you wander down the smaller side streets you will find wonderful little places with fewer tables and a more relaxed atmosphere. Look for a fabulous little piazza with a trattoria where you can sit outside and take in the view while enjoying a pasta meal to-die-for!

5. BREAK YOUR RULES.

At home I never eat pasta, but when I'm in Italy I eat it often. Another of my favorite places in Rome is **A Casa Mia**, on a little street in the neighborhood I stay in, with four or five other restaurants and trattorias all facing a little piazza. The owner seats us at one of the six tables on the sidewalk and advises us what to order.

Last time I was there (with a small group of my Glam Italia women) he suggested we have the carbonara. I wasn't in the mood for pasta, and definitely not carbonara, which I always think of as dense and heavy, but the owner is good fun and totally engaging, so we all did as we were told and ordered the carbonara. I can't begin to describe how amazing it was! The homemade pasta had been made that day in the restaurant's kitchen, and the carbonara was light but delicious, just coating the pasta, not drowning it.

The conversation at our table stopped. All four of us were so overwhelmed by this insanely fantastic food we literally couldn't speak. All we could do was eat as slowly as humanly possible, breaking only to sip the house wine, which was also wonderful.

The women from that tour still talk about that pasta! Not only was it a meal to write home about and a story to tell forever, but each bowl of pasta cost 8 euros and the wine was 4 euros. You honestly don't have to break the bank in Italy to have a sensational meal.

Italian Courses

Beware – the servings will be enormous! Order less than you think you need. Even though the bread will be fantastic, you may want to skip it.

1. ANTIPASTO

The first round of food is antipasto. Personally, that's all I normally need (but need and want are different things...). Antipasto is typically some **cold meats like prosciutto and mortadella, olives, artichoke hearts, pickled vegetables and cheeses.** Every eatery will have its own antipasto and no two will be the same. If you are a seafood-lover and are anywhere along any of the coastlines, seafood antipasto is to die for!

2. PRIMO PIATTO

The next course is called Primo or Primo Piatto. This course is hot and frequently is meat-free. This is the **pasta, polenta or risotto** dish. You may also be served **gnocchi** or **soup** in the primo course.

3. SECONDO PIATTO

After the Primo comes the Secondo Piatto course, offering cuts of **meat, chicken and fish**. If you are having a steak or roasted meat they will be served during the secondo.

Contorno

Contorno is a **side dish selection** commonly offered at the same time as the secondo piatto and is normally vegetables.

4. INSALATA

Typically, this will be a form of **house salad**. If the vegetable in the contorno course was a leafy green, you may not see a salad course.

5. FORMAGGI E FRUTTA

Formaggi e Frutta will be a selection of **local cheeses** (local to that town or region, not local in the broader sense of just being Italian cheese) and **seasonal fruit**.

6. DOLCE

This meal is still not done! The dolce or **sweet** course is served next. This might be tiramisu, gelato, cake, panna cotta or whichever desserts are from that region.

7. CAFFE

After the meal comes **coffee**, but not milky coffee like cappuccino, this is time for an espresso. Italians don't drink cappuccino beyond breakfast and don't drink anything milky after a meal.

8. DIGESTIVO

After all that food you need a digestive to ease your digestion. This is when **grappa, limoncello and amara** are served. Often if you ask for a limoncello, the waiter will just bring a bottle and some glasses to your table. They won't charge you for the whole bottle, if they even charge you at all.

Obviously, you don't have to order all these courses. I usually order only one course, because I simply cannot eat that much!

Dining Out Basics

COPERTA

Your bill may include a coperta or cover charge per person. This covers the cost of the bread and is normally around 2 euros per person. The menu should state that there is a coperta.

SERVIZIO

This is something you generally see only in tourist restaurants. It is a service charge percentage of the total bill.

TIPPING

Italians don't usually tip and it is not necessary, but if I have had good service I still feel compelled to tip. My Italian friends tell me not to, and not to leave the 10–20% that is customary at home in the US, but I often leave something.

SITTING OR STANDING

If you stop at a coffee bar you will see two prices, one for sitting at a table and another for standing at the bar, Italian-style. Italian coffees are short and strong (and is the best coffee ever!) so coffee is consumed relatively quickly. Standing at the coffee bar chatting with friends, co-workers, other Italians, is part of the social fabric of Italy.

In most places you won't find coffee to takeaway and you definitely won't find the 20oz/600ml "venti" coffees that you see at Starbucks. You seldom see Italians walking down the street eating or drinking at all. It is just not part of their culture.

FAST FOOD

Although you will see the occasional American fast food chain restaurant in the tourist areas, fast food is not part of Italian culture either. You will see predominantly American tourists eating in these places.

I always think that if you are in the pickpocketing business, or wanting to do harm to Americans, where better than in an American fast food restaurant in a busy tourist area? Should you decide you cannot survive without a burger and fries, at least be vigilant. Be aware of everyone around you. Keep your hand on your bag at all times. (See **Chapter20 – Pickpockets** for more details.)

ASK FOR HELP

Italian food is regional, so ideally you will order the food from the region you are visiting. Don't order something because it is the only thing on the menu that you recognize. In most places your waiter will have some understanding of English, so you can ask him what he recommends, or what is a typical dish from that region. You can also use a translator app on your smartphone to help identify the different ingredients.

EAT LOCAL

Most non-tourist restaurants will serve fresh pasta instead of boxed pasta, and most menus revolve around foods that are in season and that have been grown nearby. In the US, many of the vegetables and fruits we eat ripen in the back of a truck as it drives across the country. In Italy, most of what you eat has come from within a few miles radius of where you are. It's sustainable eating at its best!

Imposters

Some food that we think of as Italian food is in fact not Italian. You won't find these on the menu in an Italian restaurant in Italy:

Caesar Salad. Caesar salad is actually Mexican. Caesar Cardini invented the salad in Tijuana.

Spaghetti and Meatballs. Meatballs were added to pasta by Italian immigrants to America. After a lack of meat in Italy there was an abundance of affordable meat in America and as such meatballs were added to pasta.

Garlic Bread. Not in Italy!

Chicken or Veal Parmigiana. You will find *Eggplant* Parmigiana, but not the others.

Pepperoni Pizza. *Pepperoni* in Italian actually translates to *large bell peppers.* Pizza in Italy is very different from pizza in America: usually the pizza base will be thin, there will be little tomato sauce (if any) and it won't be sweet, there will not be loads of cheese, just a little, and the toppings will be different too.

Mozzarella Sticks. Nope. Not Italian.

Italian Dressing. Salad dressing in Italy is oil and vinegar. That's all. You won't find the American version of Italian dressing, or Ranch, Thousand Island, Blue Cheese etc.

Mind Your Manners

Sit and watch a table of Italians eating and you might be surprised at their table manners. Italians don't talk with a mouthful of food, or even speak at all with food in their mouths, and they don't eat with their mouths open.

Italians use their cutlery for almost everything they are eating, and they use it correctly.

So, be aware of your table manners. Eat with your mouth closed and don't speak with food in your mouth. When in Rome, do as the Romans do!

CHAPTER FIFTEEN
Italian Food by Region

There is more than one Italian cuisine.

As I have said, Italian food is regional. Everything food-related changes based on where in Italy you are. Typically, you will find that everything on the menu is in season and has been grown not far from where you are. (Another detail that I personally love is that, unlike America, there are no GMOs in the food in Italy.)

In some areas, pasta is a staple part of the local diet, in others it isn't. How pasta is made (before any sauces get involved), what type of wheat is used, whether egg is added or not, even the pasta *shape* changes by region. From the ear-shaped *orecchiette* pasta you find in Puglia, to the wide, flat *pappardelle* they serve in Tuscany, the shape of a pasta or noodle is dependent on the type of sauce it is served with. The sauces themselves are also entirely regional. You won't find lasagna on the menu everywhere, nor will you find spaghetti carbonara, spaghetti Bolognese, or even fettucine in every place you go.

As much as we think of pizza as being an Italian food, you don't want to order it everywhere. In Venice they don't have wood-burning ovens, so you may not want to order pizza there. In Liguria they eat focaccia rather than pizza. Pizza comes from Naples, and Naples has the best pizza in the world!

Some of the foods listed below are my personal favorites, some is food I have researched to try next time, and other foods are recommendations from friends who live in Italy, who have messaged me late at night with items that *had* to be included! I hope these will serve as a starting point for you and encourage you to try as many different, regional foods as possible while in Italy.

AOSTA VALLEY

Due to the cold, alpine climate, the food of the Aosta Valley tends to be hearty, featuring filling rice, polenta and gnocchi dishes, heavy soups, black breads and dairy products. Fontina cheese comes from this region and is the base of numerous local fondues.

Risotto alla Valdostana is a hearty rice dish with fontina and parmesan cheeses. *Polenta alla rascard* uses cold slices of polenta layered with beef and sausage ragu and fontina cheese. Keep an eye out for *Bosses de Jambon*, a ham seasoned with local mountain herbs.

ABRUZZO

Maccheroni all Chitarra is a local pasta, made by rolling sheets of pasta through a frame strung with what look like guitar strings. The pasta is served with local sauces made from goose, pork or lamb. *Scripelli* crepes are served in soup or made into souffles with ragu, chicken livers, meatballs and local sheep's milk cheese. *Gnocchi carati* is served with a sauce made from sheep's milk cheese, bacon and eggs.

Make sure you try *arrosticini* (skewered lamb served with *bruschetta*), *brodetto* (a fish stew), *fegato* (liver) and *ventricina* (a delicatessen/cold cut meat made from cured fatty pork).

BASILICATA

Basilicata has two short coastlines, one to the west on the Tyrrhenian Sea, the other to the south on the Ionian. The bulk of this region is mountainous and has a rich agricultural history. Olives, vegetables and legumes are grown here, as well as wheat for pasta.

Local dishes feature a lot of pork, vegetables and chili peppers, such as *Cutturiddi* (a meat and vegetable stew). Basilicata claims to be the first region to cook *salsiccia* sausage. Another popular sausage to try is *lucanica. Senise peppers* find their way into many of Basilicata's foods.

A pignata is a traditional clay urn-like pot used for cooking dishes such as *Pignata di Pecora* (lamb with potatoes, tomatoes, pork and pecorino) and *Spezzatino di Agnello* (lamb with potatoes, onions and peppers). The ingredients are layered inside the urn and a pastry-style lid is placed over the opening, before it is left to cook for hours in the fireplace.

Orecchiette con salsa picante is pasta shaped like little ears with a tomato sauce and spicy local salami.

Lagane is a dish that dates back to the Roman rule, and is made with walnuts, beans, chickpeas and soft bread.

Most sauces start with a base of olive oil, garlic and pepperoncino.

Two other must-try foods in Basilicata are *Ciaudedda* (braised artichokes stuffed with fava beans, onions, potatoes and salted pork), and the delicious *Focaccia a Brazzudo* which is made with pork crackling, lard and oregano.

Regional cheeses are frequently made from sheep's milk. Look for *Caciocavallo Podolico, Butirro, Pecorino di Filiano, Cacioricotta, Canestrato di Moliterno* and *Manteca.* Paired with a loaf of local Matera bread, some olives and a bottle of Aglianico, any of these cheeses will round out a perfect picnic.

CALABRIA

Calabrian cuisine has a *cucina povera* (peasant food) tradition and incorporates the food of the land and the sea with a giant serving of chili peppers! Spicy sausage like *Njuda,* which can be served with bruschetta or in pasta, will set your taste buds on fire, but it is fantastic! *Caciocavallo* cheese (cheese on horseback) is distinctive not only in its salty, sharp flavor but also for the teardrop shape it makes when hung to dry. It is great with cold meats and hearty Calabrian red wine, as well as cooked in pasta dishes.

Lagane e Cicciari is a simple but wonderful dish made with wide, flat noodles, chickpeas, garlic and olive oil.

Pasta ccu ri sarde is an ancient Arabian dish made with locally-caught sardines. It is a sweet and salty pasta with pine nuts and raisins and is not to be missed!

Piscispata a 'gghiotta is a swordfish dish with tomatoes, olives, onions and capers.

Rigulizza is a local licorice that is world-renowned, and *struffoli,* or *pignolata,* is a fried honey confection that made its way from Sicily and is popular at Easter and Christmas.

CAMPANIA

Campania is the home of pizza – the very best pizza in the world! A slice of *pizza Margherita* (the simplest pizza made with mozzarella, tomato and basil) is an absolute must. The thin base makes it lightweight enough that it is normal to have a whole pizza to yourself.

Caprese salad is from Campania, as is *mozzarella di bufala* (buffalo mozzarella) which comes from the farms south of Salerno.

Spaghetti alle vongole (pasta with clams) and *pasta alla puttanesca* (capers, oregano, garlic, black olives and tomato) are great local pastas to try, and pretty much *anything* with seafood is a must.

In Naples, make sure you try the coffee – it is the very best in all of Italy – and try the *Baba*, a rum-flavored sponge cake. *Sfogliatella* is a layered pastry, filled with ricotta, egg, cinnamon, sugar and orange.

Sorrento lemons and Amalfi lemons not only perfume the region but also find their way into both food and drink – this is the home of *limoncello*! Sixty percent of the Sorrento lemons are used to make limoncello.

EMILIA-ROMAGNA

Just an hour north of Florence by train, this region is considered to have some of the best cuisine in all of Italy.

Parmesan cheese, *prosciutto di parma* and aged balsamic vinegar all come from Emilia-Romagna. This is also the home of stuffed pastas – *lasagna, ravioli, tortellini, tortelloni* and the tomato and ground meat sauce we know as *Bolognese*.

Crudo is an Italian version of Japanese sashimi, or sliced raw fish, found along the coast.

Further inland, the ubiquitous truffle (*tartufo*) and chestnuts (*castagne*) flavor many dishes in this region.

Piadine (flatbread sandwiches) are a common lunch or snack food, especially with prosciutto and cheese. Emilia-Romagna is famous for rich pasta dishes, but some other lunch items to try are *crescentina* (deep fried breads) *erbazzone* (a pie made from savory greens) and *cappellacci* (pumpkin-stuffed ravioli).

FRIULI-VENEZIA GIULIA

This region has a strong Austrian and central European influence in both its cuisine and culture. The region shares a long border with Slovenia and it also stretches along the Adriatic. The cuisine is rich in polenta, which ties it to the Veneto, but also soups with dumplings instead of pasta, which tie it to central Europe.

Some soups to keep an eye out for include *Bobici* (made from ham, beans, corn and potatoes), *Boreto alla Graisana* (a turbot chowder with olive oil, vinegar and garlic), and the Germanic *jota* (made from sauerkraut, sausages, potatoes and beans with sage and garlic).

Inland, stews made with venison and rabbit in a wine sauce called *salmi* are popular, as is *goulash* (a beef stew with hot peppers, onions and tomatoes). Stews are served with polenta.

Bauletti are individual stuffed pastas that look like little trunks and are filled with ham and cheese, veal and spinach.

Along the coast, seafood is a big part of the local cuisine, especially turbot, sardines, shrimp, scallops and cod. *Risotto di Marano* is made with shrimp, mussels and squid, and *Granzevola alla Triestina* is made with spider crab and bread seasoned with lemon, garlic and parsley.

Friuli is also known for its *salumi*, with the much sought-after *Prosciutto di San Daniele, Prosciutto de Sauris* and *Prosciutto Carsolino*. *Muset* is a sausage made from pork shin, snout and skin to be eaten with a horseradish-based condiment, or *brovada*, which is a pickled turnip dish akin to sauerkraut. Here, goose meat is also used to make sausage, as is goat and pork.

The most important local cheese is *Montasio*. The salty *Carnia*, along with *Tabot* and *Latteria* are also popular local cheeses.

Frico are savory cheese wafers made with *Montasio* cheese and *paparot* (a cornmeal mixed with garlic and spinach).

Other foods to look for include chestnut cookies called *Castagnoli*, pumpkin fritters called *fritulis*, and *chifeleti* cookies made from potato-enriched dough.

LAZIO

When in Rome you must try *suppli*, one of the city's best street foods. Rice or risotto balls are stuffed with a piece of mozzerella and some tomato based ragu, soaked in egg, bread-crumbed and then fried to perfection.

Another personal favorite in Rome is *carciofi* (artichokes). If you go to the Jewish Ghetto you can try *Carciofi alla Giudia* (Jewish artichokes), which are deep fried like potato chips, or *Carciofi Romana,* which are regular steamed artichokes served with a dipping sauce.

Lazio is the home of carbonara served with fresh spaghetti, but also look for *Bucatini all'Amatriciana* (thin pasta tubes with spicy pork sauce), and *Penne all' Arrabbiata* (a spicy tomato pasta sauce, seasoned with chili peppers and garlic). *Cacio e Pepe* is a cheese and pepper pasta that illustrates the simplicity of the food in Lazio.

LIGURIA

Liguria stretches along the coast of the Italian Riviera. The mild climate here is perfect for growing olives, grapes and vegetables, so the local cuisine is known for the simple flavors of local produce, especially the local pesto!

Liguria is the home of *pesto alla Genovese,* made from fresh basil, local olive oil, pine nuts, garlic and Parmigiana Reggiano. A plate of the local *trofie* pasta with pesto is a must while in Liguria. Another popular local dish is *pansouti con salsa di noci* (pasta pockets stuffed with ricotta, chervil, chicory and herbs served in a walnut sauce with grated Parmigiana Reggiano).

It is said that ravioli was invented here in Liguria. Whether true or not, they say that at the end of a meal onboard ships the leftover food would be chopped up, mixed together, packed into pasta parcels and served at the next meal.

Ligurian cuisine is full of fabulous seafood options, with seafood featuring more predominantly than red meat on most menus.

Minestrone is thought to have originated here, and the seafood soup *cioppino* is based on the Ligurian *ciuppin* soup. This original version was created by fishermen using fish that were too small or not sellable, so they would slow cook them and make them into a delicious soup. (The American-style cioppino has a lot more tomato than the original.)

Instead of ordering pizza while in Liguria, a savvy traveler would order focaccia. Did you know that focaccia is 2000 years older than pizza? From plain focaccia with olive oil and salt, to focaccia with herbs, to *focaccia di recco* (made with local cheese from Recco), no trip to Liguria is complete without at least trying this local delicacy. Try to have just one slice!

Farinata is a street food flat pancake made from chickpeas, often served with olive oil and local herbs, and best eaten piping hot.

LOMBARDY

The cuisine in Lombardy is rich and heavy and uses a lot of dairy products.

In Lombardy, polenta and rice are eaten far frequently than pasta. *Risotto alla Milanese* is a decadent, creamy, golden-hued rice dish, colored by the most expensive herb in the world, saffron. It is served with dairy butter and *Parmigiano Reggiano* cheese. Not all rice dishes are risottos though, *Risott' Rusti* is a rice dish made with pork and beans and *Risott' alla Pilota* is a simple rice and sausage dish. Rice is also used in soups.

Although pasta is not a staple in Lombardy, there are some interesting pasta dishes to look for. One of them is *tortelli de zucca*, a pasta pocket filled with crushed almond cookies, *mostardo* (a mustard flavored candied fruit), winter squash and grated cheese, and served in a sauce of melted butter and sage.

Casoncelli are stuffed pasta crescents filled with a mixture of sausage, garlic, parsley, breadcrumbs, egg and cheese and served in a creamy sauce with butter and sage.

Meat and poultry are an important part of the Lombardia cuisine. Veal is used in many recipes including: *Costoletta alla Milanese* (breaded veal cutlets fried in butter and served with a splash of lemon juice), *Osso Buco Milanese* (slowly simmered veal shanks), *Uccelli Scappati* (skewered veal and pork with fresh sage), *Vitello Tonnato* (cold roasted veal sliced and served with a sauce made from capers, lemons, anchovies and tuna).

Goose meat is used to make foie gras, sausages and salami.

Local cheeses to look for include *Gorgonzola, Grana Padano, Provolone Padana, Valtellina Casera, Bitto, Taleggio* and *Parmigiano Reggiano.*

At Christmas, the famous *panettone* cake is served here. More of a sweet, egg-based bread than cake, it has raisins and citron, is light textured and often served with panna (cream).

LE MARCHE

If you are on the coastal side of le Marche, look for *brodetto* (a fish soup with a variety of seafood in a tomato and onion base).

The inland side of Le Marche is famous for *porchetta* (a garlic and fennel flavored boned roast of pork).

MOLISE

Along the coast, fish dishes prevail, such as *Baccala' con le Patate* (roasted cod with potatoes). Inland, *Cavatelli al sugo d'agnello* is a style of Molisean pasta in a lamb and tomato sauce.

PIEDMONT

Piedmont is famous for its tannin-heavy Nebbiolo wines and is also touted as both Italy's food capital and it's most culinarily-progressive region. This is where the Slow Food Movement began.

The area is world-renowned for its beef, and also the famous white Alba truffle, *Tartufo Bianco d' Alba*. The best time of year to enjoy the white truffle is November.

Piedmont is *grissini* country and you will find them everywhere you eat! These long, thin, crunchy bread sticks are fabulous with local cheese and a glass of Barolo.

Bagna Cauda (hot bath) is a local staple. This is a fondue made with anchovies, garlic and olive oil, kept hot with a flame underneath, with roughly-chopped local vegetables dipped into it. Once upon a time it was the traditional appetizer to start the evening meal. Perfect with autumn vegetables, it is so much a part of the local culture that it has its own three-day festival every November.

Tajarin is one of the most traditional pastas in Piedmont. It is cut into long, thin quarter inch (half-centimeter) ribbons, similar to tagliatelle. The rich Piedmontese farmhouse eggs used to make Tajarin give it a deep golden color. The two main ways to enjoy this pasta are either with a tomato-based meat sauce or with the classic Piedmont melted butter and sage sauce.

Another pasta to try is *Agnolotti del Plin* (tiny ravioli stuffed with veal, pork, beef, rabbit or vegetables and pinched closed – plin means pinch), again served with either a meat sauce or with butter and sage.

Carne cruda is raw Piedmont beef. This special type of cow has very little fat and a double layer of muscle and is apparently incredibly tender. (I don't eat red meat, so haven't tried this one.) Carne cruda is supposed to be fantastic, but be prepared for it to be served raw, either ground or in fine slices.

Brasato is braised beef. The famous Piedmont beef is also marinated overnight in local Nebbiolo wines, hearty red Barolo or Barbera and then braised. Again, it is said to be delicious.

There are many cheeses from this dairy rich region, but one to try here is *Castelmagno*. It is made from milk from Piedmontese cattle who live on fresh hay and pasture in the Piedmontese meadows. Castelmagno is eaten many different ways and in many different foods but is wonderful by itself with a glass of Barolo or drizzled with local honey.

PUGLIA

Puglia is like nowhere else in Italy. A mere 45 miles (72 kilometers) from Greece it actually looks more Grecian than Italian with its whitewashed little towns overlooking its incredibly blue oceans, the Adriatic and the Ionian. Puglia grows olives and grapes and is known for its huge volume production of olive oil and wine, and for its wheat. Protein-rich durum wheat is used to make bread that is popular all over Italy. Make sure you try Altamura bread while you are there.

The high-protein durum wheat doesn't require eggs to make it into pasta. (In other regions eggs are added to increase protein.) *Orecchietti* pasta is perhaps the region's most famous, shaped by hand into "little ears". You must try it at least once with its signature *Crime de Rape* sauce, made from turnip tops. It is fantastic.

Other local pastas include *cavatelli*, *stacchiodde* and *troccoli*. Pastas are served with aged ricotta, grano arso (a nutty flavored burnt grain) white beans (cicerchie), mussels (cozze), zucchini flowers, wild fennel, and chicory. Food here is simple but absolutely incredible!

Fava beans have been a staple food here for centuries. *Fave e cicoria* is a garlicky fava bean mash with fresh chicory.

Panzerotti are small, fried calzone-like pockets filled with olives, tomatoes, onions and pecorino cheese.

With somewhere around 800 kilometers (500 miles) of coastline, seafood is a big part of the cuisine in Puglia. Fresh and plentiful, all of it is delicious, but make sure you try at least one plate of mixed seafood antipasti while you are there.

Taralli are Italy's answer to the pretzel, but so much better! These circular snacks come from Puglia and are great on their own or with a glass of local wine. *Frisella* is a dry, crunchy bread that is baked in a stone oven, it looks a little like a bagel, and is wonderful as the base for local bruschetta.

Il Rustico is a street food that is hard to find anywhere but Puglia. Similar to a calzone but made from puff pastry instead of pizza dough, the fillings vary from town to town, so you need to try a few!

There are lots of sheep in Puglia which means lots of wonderful sheep's milk cheeses. Try *Canestrato Pugliese*, named after the baskets in which it ages, and *Cacioricotta* (a seasonal ricotta). There are also cheeses made to be eaten within 24 hours, such as *Burrata di Andria*, *Fallone di Gravina*, *Caciofiore*, and *Pampanella*, which takes flavor from the fig leaves it comes wrapped in.

Pasticciotto is a creamy custard-filled flaky pastry from Lecce. You must try it.

SARDINIA

Despite being an island in the Mediterranean, Sardinian cuisine has a strong focus on products of the land. *Porceddu* is pork, roasted with myrtle and rosemary. *Malloreddus* is a pasta made with tomato sauce, sausages, onions and local pecorino cheese, *Culurgiones* are pastas filled with ricotta and mint, in a tomato sauce.

SICILY

Sicilian cuisine has many influences including Greek and Arab. The food is fresh, spicy and light. Almonds, raisins, pistachios, saffron and anchovies all make an appearance, and before you recoil in horror, let me assure you that fresh, marinated *alici* are nothing like the salty anchovies you find elsewhere. Chances are you won't realize you were eating anchovies until you try to order more!

Arancini are cone-shaped fried rice balls filled with ragu.

Start your morning with *fico d'india* (cactus fruit) or an almond granita with a fresh, warm brioche.

Pasta con le sard is a sardine-based pasta dish not to be missed.

Caponata is an eggplant dish with pine nuts and raisins.

176

Gambero rosso (red prawns from Mazara del Vallo) are eaten raw and are considered to be the best prawns in the world.

Pasta alla Norma is made with tomatoes, eggplant and salted ricotta. *Couscous di pesce* is a dish of fresh fish on a bed of couscous.

Cannoli filled with ricotta are a Sicilian staple dessert.

Basically, everything you can find to eat in Sicily is completely amazing.

TRENTINO-ALTO ADIGE

The cuisine here is a mixture of Italian and Germanic influences, a little Mediterranean and a little mountain cooking. Fresh water fish and game are on menus here as well as locally-cured, smoked ham called *speck*.

Spatzle are small gnocchi made with eggs and flour that are served with butter and chives.

Schlutzkrapfen/Mezzelune are half-moon shaped ravioli-style pasta, filled with ricotta and spinach.

Canederli are flour and bread dumplings either served in broth or with butter. They can be flavored with speck, cheese or spinach.

There are many local cheeses to choose from including *Trentigrana, Puzzone di Moena, Casolet* and *Vezzena*.

TUSCANY

Everywhere you go in Tuscany you will see taxidermized wild boars. These are *Cinghiale* (ching-GYAH-lay), they roam wild in the forests around Tuscany. In addition to being used as decoration, you will see Cinghiale on the menu *everywhere*. And it is delicious! You should order it more than once while you are in Tuscany, because every restaurant has its own way of preparing Cinghiale. Most frequently it is served with pappardalle or tagliatelle.

Pici (pea-chee) is a type of pasta found in the Siena-Pienza area and is served with many sauces, including duck in *pici al ragu d'anatra*.

Tuscans love their soups and there are many to choose from but keep an eye out for *ribollita* (a vegetable and bread soup), *Papa al Pomodoro* (a hearty tomato soup), and *Zuppa di Fagioli* (a soup made with cannelli beans).

You must eat the local *pecorino* cheeses, as well as local ricotta, especially when it is drizzled with local Tuscan honey!

Bistecca alla Fiorentina is the giant steak famous in Florence.

Panforte is a flourless cake/bread made of dried fruits and nuts, honey and spices, that comes from the Siena area. Originally it was made as a gift for nuns at Christmas, but now you see it in coffee shops from Siena to Florence, and it is a MUST! Have a slice with your cappuccino in the morning.

At the end of a meal in Tuscany, you may be served small biscotti-like cookies called **cantucci** (can-TOO-chi) to dip into small glasses of a hearty wine called **Vin Santo**.

UMBRIA

Umbrian food is rustic, hearty and traditional. Look for soups like **Zuppa di Farro** (made with farro, prosciutto, cheese, tomatoes and carrots) and **Zuppa di Lenticchie** (lentil soup) as well as dishes featuring the most prized Umbrian ingredient, the **tartufo** (truffle). Pastas with tartufo sauces and local truffle cheeses are definitely worth trying here.

VENETO

Venetian cuisine is generally light and fresh and seldom includes heavy meat dishes.

With Venice's proximity to the water, seafood is hugely popular and many of the traditional foods there are fish-based.

Fritto Misto is a must-try dish, a mixed fried seafood that is somehow light and not oily or heavy. Another famous Venetian fish dish is *Sardi in Saor* (sardines in a sweet and sour marinade). *Bigoli in salsa* is a local ropey pasta in an anchovy sauce, and *risotto al nero di sepia* is risotto cooked in cuttlefish ink.

If you are in Venice in the spring, try *moeche* (little green crabs from the lagoon), which are eaten whole, shell included.

For those who have the good fortune to be staying overnight in Venice, go *bacari-hopping*. Similar to wandering through Spain's tapas bars, here you can meander through a few bacari (bars) order an *ombre* (a small glass of wine known as a *shadow*) and a few *cicheti* (chick-ET-tee), which are bite-sized finger foods.

Unlike much of Italy, pasta is not the staple in Venice. Rice and polenta show up in almost every meal instead. Risotto features prominently on most menus. *Risi e Bisi* is rice and peas with pancetta, a dish that used to be served to the Doges.

Up in the Alps of the Veneto, *carne di cervo* (venison) is popular, as is a local cheese called *schiz*. *Pastin* is a local thick sausage that you may find sliced and fried and served with polenta or eaten in a sandwich.

The Treviso area is the home of *tiramisu*. While you're there, also look for a local cheese called *Grana Padano*.

In the Vicenza area, look for white asparagus from Bassano, *Asiago* cheese and a horseradish condiment called *Cren*.

This is my beginner's guide to Italian foods by region. It is by no means a definitive list – entire books are devoted to each region, and even they don't have every food and every detail! Each region will have its own cheeses and breads and pastas, all well worth discovering. Be adventurous!

Phones, Money
& Shopping

CHAPTER SIXTEEN
Phones & WiFi

Planning ahead is key.

It's important to be able to communicate while you're away if you need to, but you don't want to run up a massive phone bill. Do your research and make your arrangements *before* you leave home to ensure your service won't be interrupted.

You have lots of options!

Mobile Phones

Ask your cell phone carrier about their international policy.

Some carriers offer free international roaming, some charge by the day, some don't offer an international plan at all. These days, you need your phone for more than just calling home and texting while you're travelling. Your international plan will determine your data accessibility and roaming charges.

If your domestic plan offers unlimited data within your home country, that may not apply when you are overseas. My cell phone carrier in America, **Verizon**, charges me US$10 per day to access my American data plan when I am in Italy. When it runs out, the cost goes up and up and up. Some of my friends have used **T Mobile** and had free, unlimited data, phone calls and texts. I also know some people whose cell phone carriers have zero international service. Each service provider is different. Depending on your home country, there may also be different options for you. The cost of calls and texts while you are overseas can be prohibitive, and domestic fees usually don't apply. It is important to find out what your service provider will charge you and what your options are.

WiFi

If you don't have free data or if you have limited data, you may need to turn your data roaming off while away and stick to using local WiFi in coffee shops and restaurants.

Your hotel or rental villa/ apartment may have WiFi but it can be very slow, and may not have enough for everyone in your group to be online at the same time. There probably will not be enough bandwidth for streaming videos.

I prefer to prearrange access to my data plan, as well as using local WiFi wherever I can.

Another option if you need more internet access, or if there are several of you traveling together, is to buy or rent a portable WiFi device/modem/hotspot and then you'll have as much internet access as you need. Companies like **Espresso WiFi** will deliver a device to you in Italy and either collect it from you on your last day or give you a mailer to return it to them before you fly out. They charge around 6 euros per day. I haven't used this service yet myself, but I have been told it is fantastic, and the reviews I have read have been great. I am planning on using their service for my June 2018 tours.

One of my tour guide friends uses a portable modem he bought in Italy so that his travelers all have access to unlimited internet, and he buys new SIM cards as he needs them.

Some people buy a local SIM card for their own phone quite inexpensively and have great success with that, but others have told me it hasn't worked for them. If you do swap out the SIM card in your phone, you will have a local Italian phone number and access local data.

Normally I just use my data plan from home, which has worked perfectly for me. Whichever option you choose is going to be just fine, the important thing is to choose an option *before* you leave home so that your access isn't interrupted.

Staying in Touch

I recommend downloading **WhatsApp** or **Viber** to your smartphone and have your friends and family do the same. You get free texts and calls when using either app and can easily share photos and videos at no cost, as long as you have WiFi or data access.

Beware: If you are using free WiFi in any public place (restaurants/coffee shops/hotels), don't access your banking or anything that uses your passwords. Hackers can be using that same free WiFi and access your personal information.

CHAPTER SEVENTEEN
Money Matters

Exchange rates fluctuate throughout the day, and from day to day.

You need to consider how you'll access and protect your money while you're away, and how much accessing your money is going to cost you. You can save yourself all kinds of potential problems and get a better exchange rate with a little planning and forethought.

Talk to Your Bank

Start by finding out what your bank charges to exchange money. Sometimes when I have been in Italy the euro has been worth US$1.48, which means it cost US$1.48 to buy 1 euro. Other times it has been as good as US$1.05 (and I could buy more euros for my US dollars). There is no way of knowing ahead of time what the exchange rate will be. Today as I am writing this, 1 euro costs US$1.10.

Your bank's rate will always be higher than the official exchange rate, plus they add their own fees. Ask what they will charge you to use a foreign ATM, and what they will charge you to use your credit card internationally. The fees add up quickly and can cost you considerably.

Getting Cash

Generally, the best way to get money in Europe is to **withdraw your daily maximum** allowed from an ATM machine. You'll get charged a fee by your bank each time you withdraw cash, so rather than withdrawing 100 euros per day, withdraw 300 euros every three days, or whatever the maximum amount is that your bank allows.

Whether on my tours or traveling by myself, I have a rule with ATM machines: **only use an ATM that is inside a bank, and during hours the bank is open** (whenever possible). It means thinking ahead, but it is worth it. The reasons being that there is a certain vulnerability when you are standing on the street at an ATM machine, trying to decipher the commands and get your money into your purse. Non-bank ATMs and ATMs on the street are also easier for hackers to use to clone your card. It is much easier and safer to be inside a bank. Also, if you are inside a bank, during bank hours, there is someone to help you should the machine eat your card.

That happened to a friend of mine who was traveling in France on a tour. The ATM swallowed her card, it was a Sunday, and she had to get back on the tour bus and go to the next city on their itinerary, so she had no way to recover her card.

One time in Sicily when I was inside a bank, the tellers had to open the ATM machine to get someone's card out. At the time I thought how lucky the person was to have been inside the bank and during bank hours!

Many (if not all) banks in Italy have extra safety precautions at the door. Only one person can enter at a time, the first door closes and locks and then the second door opens and lets you through. Some banks have signs saying no umbrellas, no sunglasses, no hats. I love it – you definitely feel safe going inside and withdrawing your cash.

I have found that most ATM machines have the option to get the commands in English. There will be a language option with a picture of the Union Jack/British flag. Press that button and your directions will appear in English. They have multiple other language options available too, if English is not your first language.

It's a good idea to arrive in Italy with some euros in hand, (I normally bring 200 euros) in small bills. The airport ATM machines are even more expensive and due to the volume of non –European travelers coming through, also sometimes run out of money. They have the worst exchange rates, so I advise against using them. It can be difficult to break large bills in Italy, so try to get your cash in smaller denominations, ideally 50-euro bills and smaller.

Credit Cards

Depending on the credit card you use, you will be charged a foreign currency exchange fee every time you swipe the card and you will not always get a good exchange rate.

Don't use your debit card as a credit card, because the fees add up even more quickly. Think of it as being an extra $5–10 every time you swipe your debit card in a store or restaurant. It doesn't take long to spend an extra $100!

Look for credit cards that don't charge international fees. The **Barclay** cards tend to have no foreign transaction fees, as do the **Capital One** cards in America and the **Chase Sapphire** card. There are websites with lists of the best credit cards to travel with internationally, so you can research your options quite easily.

Visa and **Mastercard** seem to be the most readily accepted credit cards everywhere. Many places don't accept **American Express** and **Discover** card, so again do your research and make sure the credit cards you use are widely accepted in Italy.

Tipping

As I've already mentioned, it is not customary or necessary to tip in Italy. If you have been given good service at a restaurant, a small tip is much appreciated but not expected. After living in America for so many years I always feel compelled to tip the waiter, and Italians are so friendly and helpful it is a pleasure to do so! I have almost never had anything less than wonderful service.

In America it is normal to tip 10–20% of the bill, but in Italy it is more appropriate to just leave a few euros. Check to see if your bill has the word *servizio* on it. This is a service charge and means that a tip-equivalent has already been included in your bill.

Tour guides are the exception and should be tipped if they have given you a good experience. Plan on tipping tour guides around 10–20 euros if they have done a great job. The guides I hire for my tours go all out and do an amazing job each time, and so my travelers like to tip them well and always say that it was well-earned. Tipping in Italy comes down to *what* you feel is appropriate and *if* you feel it is appropriate.

CHAPTER EIGHTEEN
Shopping in Italy

Oh my. The shopping!

Yes, I have had shopper's remorse when I have come home from Italy. And not the mild form of shopper's remorse either. I've had the curled-up-in-the-fetal-position, sobbing, broken-hearted remorse. Never remorse over anything that I bought while away, but remorse over things that I *didn't* buy.

Italy is the most fabulous place on earth for shopping. If you take only one piece of advice from this book, let it be this: **leave a generous amount of space in your suitcase to bring home your shopping**. I am the queen of the "one-way bag". I can't even tell you how many times I have had to buy an extra bag for the journey home to bring back the treasures I have bought while in Italy. I have become adept at the luggage shuffle, maneuvering my extra bag into a carry-on bag, but sometimes I haven't planned so well and have been forced to pay the US$100 fee the airlines charge to check a second bag. In the end it has always been worth it.

Buy it NOW

Before we go any further on the subject of shopping, here is my number one rule for shopping in Italy: **If you see something you love, BUY IT. Right there and then.** If you walk around and think about it, chances are the object of your affection will be gone when you get back. Or you won't have a chance to get back. Or you won't be able to find your way back. The fabulous handbag, to-die-for shoes or can't-live-without-them ceramics won't be available in the next town you visit. Even if it's just a t-shirt, a mug or a kitchen magnet, if you want it, buy it when you see it.

Now that we understand the "Buy Now" principal, let's take a deeper look at shopping in Italy.

Made in Italy

Although there are department stores and some chain stores too, Italy is full of owner-operated shops and boutiques. In all likelihood, the ceramic bowl you are holding was made by the store owner or his family members. When you turn it over and see *dipinto a mano,* it means painted by hand. On one of my first trips to Italy I was in a ceramic shop in Praiano (Amalfi Coast) and saw *dipinto a mano Laura* on a plate I was holding. I jokingly said that I had Laura's plate and asked who Laura was. The owner shouted "Lowww-raahhh! Viene qua!" (*Laura – come here!*) and out she trotted from the back, paintbrush in hand! I bought the plate.

There are unique items to be found everywhere you go in Italy. At home I am an avid non-shopper. I hate shopping. But while I am away it is fun to pick up interesting and different things. I always buy bits and pieces to put away for Christmas presents, birthday presents and business gifts. I have gifted many leather-bound journals, pashmina-style scarves, ceramic plates and bowls, and locally-made soaps and candles. Everyone loves their gifts from Italy, and they also love knowing that I was thinking about them six months prior while I was in Florence! (Or wherever I may have been.)

Those kitschy souvenirs you see everywhere can bring you endless joy when you get home. From kitchen magnets to cups in the shape of vespas, to graphic tees to olive dishes, to tablecloths hand-painted with grapes and olives, to Venetian masks… souvenirs are reminders of your fabulous vacation.

Shop Regionally

Just as with wine and food, shopping in Italy is also regional. You may find leather jackets in Venice, but the place to buy them is Florence. That Venetian mask you find at a market in Florence? It was probably made in China and is likely to fall apart in no time at all. If you want a Venetian mask you should buy one in Venice. (From a shop, not a stall set up along the canal.)

WHERE TO BUY POPULAR ITEMS

I advise my Glam Italia travelers, friends and family to buy the following things from the following places:

Venice: Look for Venetian masks, Murano glass, handmade lace from Burano.

Milan: Fashion. Milan and Paris are the twin fashion capitals of the world, so this is the place to buy the latest trends, designer items and all out fabulous fashion!

Florence: Florence is famous for its leather. This is the place to buy leather jackets, belts handbags and shoes, as well as leather luggage. Florence also has fantastic designer outlet shopping. My favorite store in the world, the Prada outlet in Montevarchi, is only a quick train ride away.

Tuscany: I find amazing fragrant soaps in Tuscany. They hold their scent for years. At home I put them in clothes drawers and in closets to keep everything smelling lovely. I don't know anything about making soap, but I have found that the soaps I buy in Tuscany don't leave a film on the skin and don't dry the skin out. They are wonderful!

Rome: Rome has a little bit of everything. I particularly love buying gifts and souvenirs at the Campo di Fiori market.

Naples: My favorite things to buy in Naples are *presepe*, handmade figurines to put in your Christmas nativity scene. (We don't actually have a nativity scene at our house at Christmas, but I have bought some of the figurines, just because they are so beautiful!) Via san Gregorio Armeno is a world famous narrow, ancient alley built by the Greeks in the 5th century BC, lined with giant, dark palazzos that give it a slightly eerie, dusk-like light. Year round it is lit up like Christmas, and the shops that line the length of the alley make and sell fantastic *presepe*, from religious themed to celebrity likenesses to characters from folk lore and mythology.

The Amalfi Coast: I always buy lemon-scented candles, fragrance diffusers and soaps in Sorrento and Positano. This is also the home of Limoncello, the lemon-based liqueur/digestivo. Other places claim to make Limoncello, but the key ingredient is the special lemons that are grown only in this region. The Amalfi Coast area is also famous for ceramics.

Capri: Treat yourself to a pair of world famous Capri sandals. You can have them made to order while you wait or buy them ready-made. This style of sandals was worn by Romans before Christ and was also worn by celebrities such as Jackie Kennedy. Suffice to say you will be following some fascinating footsteps! Capri and Positano (across the bay) are both great places to buy fresh, summery linen and cotton clothing, and beach wraps.

Sicily: There is so much to buy in Sicily, but I am particularly partial to the ceramics. Keep an eye out for giant head ceramics as well as outdoor urns and flower pots.

Shopping in Markets

Every little town and village has its own market day once a week. This is where the local ladies do their weekly shopping. As a traveler, it is a window into a local life that is wonderful to participate in. By 7am vendors are setting up their stalls selling fruit and vegetables, all of which were grown nearby, cheeses, freshly butchered meats, fresh deli meats, fish, wine, olive oil and other foodstuffs from the immediate area. In many markets there will also be stalls with leather handbags, belts and wallets, linen clothes, other clothes and shoes, and hand-painted table linens. Some markets will have stalls selling household goods.

I spend as much time as I can in a little medieval town in Tuscany called San Gimignano. The market day there is Thursday and I always make sure I have the morning free to wander the market stalls, buy fresh fruit and vegetables, bread and local pecorino cheeses as well as prosciutto that is shaved for me as I watch. One of the vendors regularly roasts a pig on a spit the night before and sells sandwiches (panini) that are simply warm local rolls with fresh sliced pork. No condiments, no lettuce or tomato, just bread and warm pork. It is the best thing ever.

Bring Cash

Markets are all about cash. Some vendors may take debit and credit cards, but you should go there assuming no one does. Take cash in small denominations, nothing larger than a 20-euro bill. If you try to pay with a 50 they may not have enough change to give you, or you might wipe out all of their change, so they will refuse you the sale.

Non Toccare! Do Not Touch!

You may see a sign or you may just be expected to know, but **do not touch any fruit or vegetables**. Ask for three tomatoes and the vendor will hand you the next three tomatoes ready to be sold. All the fruit and vegetables were picked yesterday in order to be perfect to eat today, so everything is just-right ripe. If you reach out a hand to squeeze a piece of fruit, expect to get yelled at!

Antiques

In Italy you don't find Goodwill stores or secondhand stores, so when someone buys an old estate and wants to get rid of the furniture it came with or the treasures in the attic they will sell them at a market. This can be at the local market day, but it normally will be at a separate antiques-style market. In **San Gimignano, this often happens on a Saturday**. If you are in Tuscany and want to do some antiquing there is **a magnificent market in Arezzo every weekend** that is well worth visiting.

I once read in a Frances Mayes book that she would find old monogrammed linen sheets in immaculate condition at the market and buy them for her house in Cortona. I always look for them but have never found them myself.

My Buyer's Remorse Story

I have spent some glorious weekend days wandering the enormous Arezzo Market. I have also found some pretty incredible things at the San Gimignano Saturday market. One time a vendor had a huge selection of vintage Louis Vuitton bags from the 1970s. They were in amazing condition and had been in a trunk in the attic of a giant old home that had recently sold. The bags were priced between 70 euros and 100 euros (so less than US$120). My first thought was to buy some of them and sell them on ebay or Tradesy or one of the designer resale sites. I did some math and realized I could pay for my entire trip with the profit! For some insane reason I decided to walk around and think about it for a couple of hours. Did I really want to buy them? What if I couldn't sell them? I would have to buy yet another one-way bag to get them home… When I finally realized what a goldmine I was potentially sitting on I went back to get them and of course they were all gone. I still have never quite gotten over it! It is one of my most sincere shopper's remorse experiences ever. I consider myself somewhat of a pro at spotting fake Louis and at determining the real ones. These were definitely real.

Which brings me to my next piece of advice…

Don't Buy Counterfeit Designer Goods

I cannot emphasize this strongly enough. *Do Not Buy Counterfeits!* In any town that gets a decent volume of tourism you will see men on the streets and bridges with large sheets covered in designer handbag knockoffs, all lined up perfectly. **Don't stop, don't look, don't make eye contact.** If you do, they will chase you down the street to try and make a sale. Why are the bags on a sheet? When the police head their way the bag sellers will scoop up the corners of the sheet, tie up their counterfeit bags and disappear into the shadows.

In the last decade I have been seeing primarily African immigrants selling the counterfeit bags. They escape their homeland to chase a new life in Europe, and wind up stuck inside this scam. I was told that they live in shacks and on concrete floors in warehouses, in terrible conditions. They have to lease the counterfeit bags and pay back the lessors with interest. It is a no-way-out situation. The bags themselves are frequently made by children in Chinese factories. The children work insanely long hours, sitting on concrete floors, in completely deplorable conditions and get paid a pittance. I have also read that the money made from counterfeit designer goods is frequently used to fund terrorism. (If you want to be truly horrified, google the Harpers' Bazaar article on counterfeit bags. If that doesn't stop you from wanting a counterfeit, chances are you have no soul.)

Be aware that purchasing counterfeit designer goods in Italy is illegal. If you are caught (be it on the street or at the airport) you have just committed a serious crime in a foreign country and you can expect a world of trouble, as well as a 10,000 euro fine. Your embassy won't get you out of that one.

Several years ago, I had a friend who told me the story of buying a perfect replica of a Gucci handbag from one of these street vendors in Florence. The bag was gorgeous, and it cost only 100 euros so she thought it a crazy good bargain. She didn't really think through the counterfeit aspect, as everyone at home was buying knock off bags at the time. Her fake Gucci was packed in her suitcase and made it through security at Florence airport, but set off the drug dogs at New York's JFK airport when she landed. It turned out her counterfeit bag was coated in cocaine dust! She didn't get fined but her ordeal with customs and drug agents at JFK was terrifying. On top of having the kind of airport experience you never want to have, missing her connecting flight out of New York (and the domino effect of problems that set off), the bag was then confiscated by the customs and drug agents.

Don't buy counterfeits.

What to Look For

When shopping in Italy, especially in markets and at market stalls on the streets of big tourist cities such as Florence and Rome, you will find some incredible merchandise and some fabulous bargains. There will be some products that are made in Italy and others that are cheap knock-offs made in China. It can be hard to tell the difference, especially if you are in a hurry. Vendors know that if you are on a cruise or a bus tour you only have a short amount of time to see everything and to do your shopping, so you are a little more vulnerable.

San Lorenzo market in Florence is my favorite street market. I have bought leather luggage there, many leather handbags, silk ties, belts, wallets, leather-bound journals and of course, leather jackets. One of my dearest friends in the world, Jimmy, has a shop at the San Lorenzo market called Jimmy's Leather Collection, and he taught me some of the ins and outs of buying leather goods:

MADE IN ITALY?

Be aware that most pieces will be stamped with an Italian leather label, and the leather is in fact from Italy, but not all the garments are *made* in Italy. You don't want to get home and find that your new leather jacket is falling apart or bleeding color onto your clothes, as some of the knock-offs will. The label *Fatto in Italia* means *Made in Italy*. Always look to see that your garment was actually made in Italy. Look too at the stitching on your garment. Have the seams been glued instead of stitched, or are the edges left rough? The stitching should be clean and straight. Check the lining of your garment, make sure it sits smoothly and isn't bunched up at the seams or where the sleeves meet the body. Your jacket should be lined – lining helps it to hold its shape. Also look at details of the cuffs, the collar and the shoulders. A well-made jacket will have smooth transitions. A cheaply made knock-off will often be bunchy at the shoulders or have chunky joins at the collars or cuffs.

Well-made Italian leather jackets can be very affordable, so don't be tricked into buying something just because it's cheap. At Jimmy's leather shop, they use vegetable dyes that are non-toxic, and that don't bleed onto your clothing. As such, I can wear my red leather jacket over a white sundress and not have any color transfer. If you follow me on Instagram you will have seen my red leather jacket showing up in various places around the world. It is the anchor piece in my wardrobe, and my absolute favorite piece of clothing.

Labels to Look For

Fatto In Italia Made in Italy

Fatto a Mano Handmade

Dipinto A Mano Hand-painted

Sconti Sale!

Shipping Goods Home

There are two ways to look at getting your surplus goodies home if your suitcase is full. There is the aforementioned **one-way bag** that can cost you US$100 in excess baggage if you have to check it, and there is **shipping goods home**. I have done both.

When I have had to pack for rainy and cooler weather in late May, but was staying through the hot weather at the end of June/early July, I have shipped my cool weather clothes and shoes back home part way through my trip. I have used both **Mail Boxes Etc** and the **postal service** in the past to do this, and both have been great. My box of clothes arrived home ahead of me and it cost around 50 euros to get it there.

If you buy wine or olive oil while you are in Italy (and I recommend you do), you need to think about how you are getting them home. You need to know your country's policy on bringing liquids into the country, and also what the alcohol allowance is. Remember, in America, if you have a connecting flight and you have bottles of wine or oil in your carry-on luggage, it will be confiscated.

So long as you are within your country's limits and have good packaging, you can pack bottles in a suitcase that is being checked in. Only do this with a sturdy suitcase. Know that baggage handlers throw suitcases and stack heavier suitcases on top of them, so a flimsy suitcase is likely to result in broken bottles.

These days I always pack bubble wrap in my suitcase in case I want to bring back a bottle of something, but other times I have wrapped the bottle in clothing and secured it somewhere safe inside my bag and it reached home in one piece.

The other option is to have the winery ship your purchases home for you. On my tours, we regularly ship home bottles of wine from the wineries we visit. They package the wine securely, insure it and ship it. The price seems to average around 90 euros per 12 bottles and in my opinion is worth every penny.

Clothes and Shoes

Italy has to be the best place in the world to buy clothes and shoes. I love finding boutique shoe shops where the owner is also the shoemaker. There is something exciting about buying handmade Italian leather shoes. One of my travelers in 2017 bought multiple pairs of handmade shoes in Florence. They were beautiful, well made, and completely different from anything I have seen available here in the US. Make sure you try shoes on before you buy them – the sizing is different than in non-European countries.

GETTING STYLED

You will notice that Italians, regardless of their income bracket, dress with an incredible sense of style. You don't see the women schlepping around in sweats or yoga pants and you don't see the men in cargo shorts and graphic tees. They always look stylish, and as a nation they seem to take pride in their appearance.

Buying clothes in Italy is a fabulous experience, especially for girls and women who don't have model-like bodies. Be prepared for the sales person to be brutally frank with you. She won't be scared to tell you not to even consider wearing that color, or that the item you are holding wasn't designed for your body. Right when you are about to shrink away just mortified she will pull clothes off the rack and tell you how gorgeous you will look in *this* color, and that hips like yours need to be swinging down the street in *this* shaped skirt!

Italian women are raised to appreciate their femininity and to acknowledge what they've got rather than try to hide the bits they don't like. When you walk into a clothing store the sales person sizes you up in a second, sees your best features and knows how to play them up. He or she won't just bring you clothes but will *style* you. It's the greatest thing ever! You walk away from the experience not only with some new clothes, but feeling like a million dollars, no matter at which price point you were shopping.

Nespresso

If you are a Nespresso drinker, it's a great opportunity to stock up on Nespresso coffee pods while you are in Italy. They are half the price of Nespresso in America, and less expensive than in most other non-European countries. The sales associates are still appropriately snooty, which I find madly entertaining. (Why is this universally the case with Nespresso? In every Nespresso store I have been to anywhere in the world the sales associates have been rude and high-handed. Perhaps in some weird way, it adds to the charm?) They also frequently have flavors unavailable in the US.

Getting the Sales Tax Back

In Italy there is a 20% VAT, or Value Added Tax, built into the price of everything. In the US, sales tax is a separate entity that is added to the item cost, and the sales tax rate varies from city to city. If something costs 10 euros in Italy, that is the amount you pay. If an item costs $10 in America, it's anyone's guess what the final price will actually be.

AT THE STORE

You can't claim the VAT you've paid on hotel accommodation or rental cars, nor for any small expenses, but when you spend 155 euros or more at a single store you can claim back the VAT you have paid. (The rules around the exact dollar figure spent and the percentage VAT may change.) The business must be set up with the appropriate paperwork and not all stores are prepared for it, but many or most tourist stores are. Some will have a sign in the window advertising that you can get VAT refunded.

If you are in a big store, such as the Prada Outlet in Montevarchi, they will have tax forms for you when you pay for your goods. They will need your passport and will fill out most of or all of the information on your tax form for you. I recommend going over everything with them before leaving the store, just to make sure you have all the necessary paperwork.

AT THE AIRPORT

Get to the airport early because you will need to go to the local customs desk and wait in line, sometimes for ages. In big, busy airports it can take a while. Customs will stamp your paperwork and sometimes will look at the items you have purchased. The items you are claiming are supposed to be unused and on hand for them to look at, so don't wear that new pair of Pradas before you leave the country! Once your paperwork is stamped you will go to either the **Global Refund** or **Premier Tax-Free kiosk** or desk and receive your VAT back either in cash or a credit card refund.

FOR MORE INFORMATION

You can find the most up to date information about this process by going to www.GlobalBlue.com or to www.agenziadoganemonopoli.gov.it and click on the tab for your language (English has the symbol of the British flag) and then click the tab for *Dogane*.

CHAPTER NINETEEN
Beach Life in Italy

With more than 7600 kms of gorgeous coastline to enjoy, a trip to the beach in Italy is a must!

Whether you want to lie in the sun and swim, walk along the shore or the beach promenade, or take a boat trip along the coast, beach life in Italy is wonderful!

It is also completely different from the beach experiences I had growing up. Beaches in my native New Zealand are a wild and untamed part of the great outdoors. Swimming happens only between flags erected and while watched over by lifeguards, due to dangerous currents and rips that can drag you out to sea, but there is endless space to pick a spot, throw down a towel or blanket and stake your claim. The same thing was true in Australia at all the beaches we visited on family vacations. Beaches were about space and freedom.

Not so in Italy.

The Lido

Although there are free beaches and free beach areas, the best Italian beach experience in my opinion is to go to private beach *stablimenti* or *lido*, where you pay for the use of beach chairs and sun umbrellas. Lined up like soldiers in perfect straight lines with perfectly measured spaces in between, the chairs and umbrellas are color-coded. One lido may be orange and white, the next blue and white, the third orange and green, and so on as they line their way along the beach.

At first, I thought it was crazy to have to pay to be on the beach, but now I love it.

When you arrive at your lido of choice and pay for the number of chairs and umbrellas you need, a suntanned fellow in red swim trunks (he doubles as a lifeguard) will show you to your assigned spot. Each lido has its own changing rooms and toilets, and most have a snack bar. Some have rows of little cabana-like sheds that families rent for the week or the summer or however long they need it and store their towels and sunscreen and toys and whatever other beach accoutrements they need, rather than drag them back and forth each day.

You find yourself immersed in a glorious part of Italian life as you are surrounded by families and lovers and people just enjoying a day at the beach. You also fall in love with the convenience of it all. There is no dragging deck chairs along the sand, or ice chests filled with snacks and drinks. No need to try to escape the sun when it gets too fierce – just adjust the angle of your sun umbrella. The beach chair contorts into every shape and height from lying flat to sitting upright. A snack or a cold drink is just a quick trot away along a manicured path, and you don't need to worry about sand getting in your food or drinks because the umbrella stand has a little table ledge to set them on. It's incredibly civilized!

Things to Know About Italian Beaches

Do a little research about the beaches you could visit before you leave home. Along the Mediterranean coast many beaches (though not all) are stone beaches.

The majority of the beaches I have been to from the **Riviera** to the **Amalfi Coast** have been stone and rock beaches. You may want to pack water shoes to make it easier on your feet.

Sardinia has crystal clear water and plenty of sandy beaches.

Sicily has both sandy and rocky beaches, but the only beaches I have been to in Sicily, both on the mainland and in the Aeolian Islands, with the exception of Vulcano, have had rocks and stones.

From **Salerno** at the bottom of the Amalfi Coast and along the southern coast you start to find predominantly sandy beaches.

The **Adriatic Coast** has endless sandy beaches.

Salento, at the bottom of the heel of Italy's boot has beaches known as the Italian Maldives, with warm, crystal clear water and white sand.

BLUE FLAG BEACHES

Only beaches that are the cleanest and most environmentally-friendly get awarded Blue Flag status. This status is reviewed each year, so you can assume beaches with Blue Flag designation are going to be very clean. If you're planning a beach vacation, look for Blue Flag beaches.

I try to have beach days while in Italy every summer. Whichever coast you are visiting, the views are dramatic and spectacular. The water is safe to swim in, and everywhere I have been the water and the beaches have been clean.

If you are staying near the beach or not far from the ocean I recommend hiring a charter boat with a guide and taking a trip along the coast. The scenery is beautiful and seeing everything from the water gives you such a different perspective. Most charters will also afford you the opportunity to stop and swim, weather and currents permitting.

Even when the temperature doesn't look terribly hot, be aware that the Italian sun, especially in the south, is fierce. You will come home with a glorious golden tan, but make sure you have plenty of sunscreen, a hat, and drink plenty of water!

Troubleshooting

CHAPTER TWENTY
Pickpockets

Don't be an easy target.

Unfortunately, when you are traveling anywhere in Europe pickpockets are a fact of life. In any crowded tourist attraction, be it the Eiffel Tower, La Rambla or St Peter's Square, a busy train station or the line waiting to get on a ferry, you can safely assume there will be pickpockets floating around.

They Could Be Anyone...

In the old days they looked like gypsies. On my first venture around Europe you would see these big Romany women with voluminous ankle length skirts full of secret pockets to hide your valuables in. They were instantly identifiable and therefore not much of a threat. If you saw one with a baby you would keep your distance, as one of their tricks was to toss the baby to you so that you would drop your handbag to catch it!

Today's pickpockets are much more wily. They are might look like American tourists, clergy, school teachers or just regular folk. They will take on the body language of locals or of tourists, looking a little confused, a little exhausted, and while your guard is down they will separate you from your watch, your jewelry, your cash and cards without you being aware of it! You can watch videos on YouTube and see them robbing money out of people's pockets and watches from their wrists without the victim even feeling it. I have heard so many people say that they would feel it if someone was getting money out of their pocket, or the wallet out of their handbag, but trust me, you probably wouldn't.

I don't tell you this to frighten you. I tell you to get your attention. I have never had a problem and I have never had anyone on one of my Glam Italia tours have a problem with pickpockets. So, without being paranoid and ruining your trip, I want you to be aware, take the necessary precautions, and then get on with enjoying your time in Italy. Put it into perspective – if you are in America and someone wants to separate you from your belongings, chances are they will have a gun. Other countries have thieves who may attack you to take your belongings. Pickpockets don't have guns and are seldom associated with violent behavior. They just sneakily take your stuff.

So, don't be an easy target. Why would a pickpocket go after someone who looks like they will be difficult to steal from when there is a sea of tourists out there not paying attention and unlikely to cause trouble?

Tips for Avoiding Trouble

LEAVE YOUR SPARKLIES AT HOME.

My first piece of advice is: leave your valuables at home. Diamond rings, expensive necklaces and bracelets, expensive watches, expensive handbags – just leave them at home. Don't wear fakes either. If a pickpocket thinks he or she spots a Rolex on your wrist, even if it turns out to be a fake, he is likely to take it and anything else he can pilfer at the same time. You don't want to give a pickpocket any reason to head your way.

STAND TALL.

Use your body language to your advantage. Square your shoulders, keep your chin parallel to the ground and walk around like you own the place. When you look confident and strong you are less enticing. There will always be other tourists looking lost or overwhelmed or walking around in circles, making themselves much easier targets. Worse still you will see other tourists standing in the middle of the sidewalk with maps open wide, clearly lost. This is like a flashing neon light to a pickpocket! Even if I am absolutely lost, I walk along as if this is my neighborhood and I'm on my way home. No one watching me would know that Siri is in my ear telling me to cross the street and turn right!

CARRY THE RIGHT BAG.

Use a cross-body handbag. A cross-body bag means you have one less thing to be watching over. Years ago, there used to be stories of boys in Naples racing past on scooters, grabbing women's handbags from their arms and disappearing into the traffic. They may be urban legend, or they may be for real – who knows? Regardless, wearing a cross-body bag means no one can snatch it.

CLOSE YOUR BAG.

Always, *always* keep your bag closed. Have it zippered shut, keep the side that opens secured against your body and keep your hand firmly on your bag *at all times*. Tote-style bags are not a good idea when traveling in Europe. They might look fantastic, but they are easy pickings for thieves who are skilled at sliding wallets, cameras and phones out of open bags.

PLAN YOUR CASH.

Separate your money. Only carry the cash you need for that particular day and don't keep all your money and all your cards in one place. Maybe keep half your cash and one card in your wallet and the other half tucked away in a deep recess inside your bag. If you are going to have cash in your pocket, keep it in your front pocket.

HIDE YOUR MONEY BELT.

Many travelers use money belts. A money belt is a flat pouch that you wear under your clothes. It can hold a passport, credit cards and cash. The idea is that you get out what you need before you leave in the morning and then don't touch your money belt all day, so no one knows it's there. When I first traveled Europe on a bus tour I wore one but haven't done since then (I was 21 at the time). If you want to use a money belt, get the kind that sits flat against your stomach, under your clothes. They now make them in breathable fabrics that don't chafe your skin or sweat. I don't recommend the type that hangs around your neck and slips under your top. I haven't used that one myself but have heard of people having the strap cut and the pouch taken.

PEOPLE-WATCH.

Know that pickpockets are seldom lone operators. They work in teams. One time in the coffee shop in the Naples train station, a barista pointed out a five-man team to me. They were spread out, watching the people they were going to rob, one going up and making conversation while the others moved around. If they were to pick someone's pocket, the barista explained to me, person number one passes the goods off to number two who hands off to number three. By the time you realize you've been robbed your things are long gone.

BE CONSISTENT.

If you are traveling in a group, everyone in the group needs to follow the rules. If one person in the group is walking around with an open handbag or flashing diamonds they will draw pickpockets to the entire group, not just themselves.

DON'T BE FOOLED.

Don't give money to beggars. This sounds really callous, I know, but much of the time they are part of a pickpocket ring. The poor impoverished woman lying on the curb begging for money breaks your heart, so you feel compelled to give her some money. Meanwhile her partner is across the street watching where you pull that money from and knows exactly where to slip their hand when they distract you or accidentally bump into you a little further down the street. You see beggars around the big cathedrals, especially St Peters in Rome, because they know you will feel like helping them is the Godly thing to do and you will likely give them money.

KEEP YOUR EYE ON YOUR STUFF...

Never put your camera or your phone or your bag down and turn away. You would be amazed at how many people do this all the time! Always keep your hands on your belongings.

...Wherever You Are.

Don't leave your handbag hanging over your chair. You will see people sitting at both indoor and outdoor restaurants with their handbag looped over the back of their chair. It takes a second for someone to slip past and lift it. Some bags, like the Travelon cross-body bags, have a carabiner clip that you can loop through the chair and fasten, so that no one can grab it. When I'm at a restaurant or sitting at a bar, I keep my handbag sitting on my foot with the handle looped over my knee. I don't ever let my bag out of my sight or off my person. It may seem a little extreme, but I have never once had my handbag taken (nor do I plan to ever let that happen).

Hang On to It.

If you are on the metro or a crowded bus or tram keep your cross-body bag worn across the front of your body and hold it firmly against your body. Public transport is a great way to get around on a budget, but it is also a great place for pickpockets to work. If you are standing by the door, make sure you have your bag strap across your body. I've read that thieves in Barcelona will wait until the last second before the door closes, grab your bag and hightail it down the platform while your train is pulling out. I don't personally know anyone who has been robbed on the metro, bus, or tram, but there are enough stories and warnings about it to make you stay aware. And remember the priest or the mom or the fellow tourist in a golf shirt standing next to you, looking like an American dad, could be a pickpocket!

Most importantly, don't let a fear of pickpockets intimidate you or ruin your trip. Be smart with your money and your belongings, be aware of the people around you, and have a wonderful time!

CHAPTER TWENTY-ONE
The Bathroom Equation

Oh, Lord.

I love Italy in all things except public toilets. Public toilets in Italy are few and far between and require a little mental preparation ahead of time. The toilet equation in your hotel room or apartment is also a little different to home, especially for those of you who live in America. So, let's prepare you to tackle toilets.

Hotel & Rental Apartment Bathrooms

Most of the buildings you will be staying in are centuries old and were built long before indoor plumbing became a thing. Consequently, you will find some very small bathrooms. Not all of them are tiny, but plenty are small by American standards.

The plumbing itself is good but was designed with narrower pipes and for less usage than we are accustomed to here in the US, and with no idea that tens of millions of tourists were only years away from finding their way to Italy. This means **you need to be careful not to clog the pipes.** Female sanitary products cannot be flushed (your apartment/villa/hotel will normally have a notice asking you not to flush them), and giant wads of toilet paper can cause pipes to get blocked up too.

FEATURES

In the bathroom, you will see two toilet-like fixtures, side by side. One is the toilet, and the second one, with faucets and a water spigot/tap is the bidet. This is not for storing ice or shaving your legs. Essentially it is a butt-washer. Need more details? Google it. (I just asked Siri and she gave me a Beyonce album, but then she has a hard time understanding my accent even with easy words!) Next to the bidet you will probably see a soap dish and a little towel rack with a bidet towel. You can Google "bidet etiquette" and find out everything you need to know about the soap and the towel and all the goings on involving the bidet. (If you intend to use the bidet you absolutely do not want to get this wrong!)

The taps or faucets in Italian bathrooms will be labeled C and F. F is for *freddo (cold* water in Italian), and C is *caldo,* which means *hot* water.

Sometimes the light switch to the bathroom or toilet may be on the wall outside the bathroom door.

Also, they don't have wash cloths in Italy. If you wish to use a wash cloth in the shower or to cleanse your face you will need to bring a couple with you from home. If you do that, I also recommend a quart-sized zip-lock bag to put damp or wet wash cloths in when it's time to pack up.

Public Toilets

Public toilets are a trickier equation. They will be referred to as *il bagno* (BAHN-yo), *la toilette* (twa-LETT-ah) or the *WC* (pronounced in English. WC stands for water closet.) Depending on the level of urgency, you can ask, *Dov'e il bagno* (doh-vay-eel-bahn-yo) or, *Il bagno per favore* (eel bahn-yo-pear-fav-oar-ray) or *Il bagno!* *Il bagno!* in an emergency.

DON'T ITALIANS PEE?

Before we go any further, understand **there aren't public toilets everywhere in Italy** like there are in America. My personal theory around the reason for this is that in Italy they really don't walk around eating and drinking. America is all about fast food and it is normal to see people there with anything from a coffee to a Big Gulp, to a cup of soda, to a bottle of water in hand as they walk down the street, sometimes eating something with the other hand too. In Italy, people generally eat sitting down at home or sitting down in a restaurant or trattoria. In America, there is a fast food joint on every corner. In Italy, fast food vendors are randomly scattered for the benefit of tourists. In America, there is bathroom on almost every corner. In Italy, there are a few public toilets, but they can be mildly terrifying if you actually manage to find one.

Be Prepared for Potential Trauma

Here are some need-to-know tips to minimize trauma when using public toilets in Italy:

TRAUMA 1.

Public toilets are frequently unisex. Not usually such a problem for the dudes, but layers of potential trauma for the girls.

TRAUMA 2.

Public toilets usually don't have toilet seats. For the life of me I don't understand why??? But on the bright side you will get gloriously strong and defined quads from squatting!

TRAUMA 3.

There often isn't anywhere to hang your handbag, and you sure as hell don't want to put it on the floor. Don't put *anything* on the floor except for your shoes. Hopefully you will have a friend to hold your handbag. And your scarf and coat and shopping bags and any other accessories you have in your hands. Only take in there exactly what you need – the stall is likely to be really small – and did I mention, don't put *anything* on the floor!

TRAUMA 4.

There may not be any toilet paper and there may not be soap or a towel to wash and dry your hands with. I sincerely recommend carrying a travel-sized pouch of baby wipes and a travel-sized pack of Kleenex with you in your handbag, just in case.

ITEM 5 (NO TRAUMA POTENTIAL BUT WORTH MENTIONING NONETHELESS).

Always have coins on hand. You may find a pay toilet, which is always a better option. The cost varies but is normally 1 euro. It is likely to be cleaner than a non-pay toilet and is more likely to have toilet paper (but good luck re the seat.) Know that if there is an attendant you will be expected to leave a tip. Make it a good one, because the toilet Gods are watching. I leave a 1-euro tip.

ITEM 6 (AND YOUR FIRST PLAN TO MINIMIZE TRAUMA).

Think ahead. Know that you may be lucky to find a toilet while you are out sightseeing and know that in any high tourist area where there *will* be a public toilet, there will most likely be a long line of other tourists waiting to use the facilities (you should also assume some of them will have bellies that haven't enjoyed the change in cuisine).

So, **use the toilet at every opportunity.** On my tours I tell my women to use the bagno at every restaurant or coffee shop we stop at, even if they think they don't need to. At first they may argue, but it only takes one urgent call of nature that requires waiting in line for a toilet stall to open, while listening to a gastric symphony playing behind that same stall door, for my travelers to see the merit in my thinking. Seriously, go to the bagno *before* going into any big tourist attraction that takes time to see, such as the Colosseum. There are toilets inside the Colosseum, but the line is always long and the smells and sounds created by masses of tourists who are not used to eating pasta can definitely be traumatic!

ITEM 7 (AND YOUR ALTERNATIVE PLAN).

The Coffee Run: if you need a bathroom just **walk into the first coffee bar you see**, order a water or a coffee and use their restroom. It probably won't have a toilet seat, and any of the aforementioned traumas may occur, but you probably won't have to wait in line, and as long as you are not in a high tourist area (such as Piazza San Marco in Venice), a coffee normally only costs 1 or 2 euros.

CHAPTER TWENTY-TWO
Plan B – What to Do When Things Go Wrong

Sometimes when you travel everything goes right. Other times, not so much.

I firmly believe that when you are traveling you have to keep a flexible mind and attitude. You also need to remember that when Plan A goes awry, invariably Plan B is much better anyway.

Sometimes you will arrive at a point of interest (museum, church, etc.) and find it inexplicably closed. You may find the trains are on strike or a hotel doesn't have your reservation. It may be pouring rain on a day you need sunshine. The boat you wanted to take along the coast may be cancelled due to rough water. There are plenty of things that *can* happen and sometimes do. The trick for not letting those things ruin your holiday is to keep cool and figure out a Plan B. I have yet to have a Plan B that hasn't turned out to be a more fantastic experience than Plan A would have been anyway!

Plan B Can Be Better than Plan A
MY VERY OWN CASERTA

One time I was staying in Salerno (at the bottom of the Amalfi Coast) and had plans to go visit the palace at Caserta, which is the largest palace in Europe and has a crazy, fascinating history. I was traveling alone, and in my mind, I had built my perfect day there: lunch in the café that looks out over the incredible gardens, renting an old-fashioned bike and riding the 3.5 kilometers to the top of the gardens and back, hours and hours to explore.

As I ran up the stairs to the platform, the train pulled away from the station without me, taking months' worth of planning with it. I went back to the ticket office and found out the next train wasn't for two hours. I was upset for a moment, but I wasn't going to miss Caserta, so I bought a new ticket and went to the wharf to walk the along the sea wall and enjoy the Amalfi Coast view for a while.

Three hours later, I reached the ticket office at Caserta. The ticket seller told me to go to the gardens immediately because they were closing soon, and to look at the royal apartments later. And this is where the Plan B travel magic began.

The bike guy wouldn't rent me a bike because he was closing in an hour, so I had to walk the gardens. There were barely any people still there, other than local Caserta residents who are allowed to ride their bikes and jog on the property. This meant I had a perfectly clear view of everything. I could photograph the length of the gardens, the statues and the fountains without bodies getting in my way! If you have ever been to any of the European palaces you will already know that this just doesn't happen. It was amazing.

Once I was done exploring the gardens, I went inside the palace to explore the royal apartments. I had researched them to death and had seen that in all the traveler photos they were full of tourists. When I walked in there at 4:30pm on a Monday in December I was the only person there. The employees who monitor the various rooms were there, so I wasn't scary alone, I was just tourist-free alone, and I had free run of the place! I could photograph the long hallways with no people in the way. I could see everything, unobstructed. In the throne room I scooted under the velvet rope and stood in the middle of the room. No one came to move me, so I lay on the floor and looked up at the frescos that cover the ceiling. They are as gaudy as all heck, but how incredible - I could see everything with a view that no one gets!

I was fascinated with Marie Carolina (Marie Antoinette's more interesting sister, who lived in the palace of Caserta) so I stopped in at the bookstore on my way out. The man working there told me that 10,000 people had come through that weekend and that the palace had been packed until about 3pm! My Plan A going wrong had turned into an incredible Plan B.

To make things even better, the bookshop man told me there was an hour before the next train to Salerno and suggested a lovely place to sit and have a glass of wine, just a short walk from the palace. He called the restaurant and told them to watch out for me, and they sent a waiter to come meet me part way there. The restaurant was in the town's circular piazza in front of the most beautiful Christmas tree I have ever seen. I sat in that beautiful place and enjoyed a glass of local wine, and when it was time to go to the train the restaurant owner told me he was sending a waiter to walk me to the station, not because it was dangerous (it wasn't) but because it was the gentlemanly thing to do!

CAR RENTAL CHAOS

Another time we had taken the ferry from the Aeolian Islands to mainland Sicily. We walked over to Hertz to pick up our rental car and found there were none! Even though we had booked a car none had come back in, not only to Hertz but to all the rental car companies in the region. People were screaming at the poor boys working behind the counter (as if it was their fault!?). Plan A was a major fail!

If you find yourself in a situation where people are behaving badly (like the people screaming at the boys), make sure you are the kind, voice of reason. I told the boys that I knew it wasn't their fault and asked them to help me. There was one car left at Catania airport, so they had it held for me. Then I needed to get to Catania, but by taxi it would be 150 euros. I needed a better option. The boys working at Hertz found a bus going from a neighboring town, and since it was closing time they volunteered to drive us there.

Plan B gave us a beautiful drive along the coast, and a private tour of Messina while we killed time until the bus was due to leave. The boys then drove us to the bus station, helped us buy tickets and get to the right bus, they loaded our bags onto the bus, talked to the driver to make sure he took care of us, and waited with us until the bus departed. We became Facebook friends and are still in contact, and Hertz got their most loyal customer in the world – me! I have never used another rental car company since, only Hertz. Plan B was fantastic!

Refer to Your List

If you always have a list of things to do that is bigger than you could ever complete, then you will always have something new to slot into the Plan B column should your initial plans for that day not pan out.

Keep Your Embassy Details On Hand

I recommend emailing yourself the address and phone number of your embassy in Italy in case you find yourself in trouble.

Should you have a car crash, be in a train crash, get caught in an earthquake or any other natural disaster, if you get arrested or if something major goes wrong, you will need to contact your country's consulate or embassy. (Before you get worried, I have been traveling the world my entire adult life and have never once had to contact my embassy. But I like to have the number handy, just in case.)

If something did happen I would want the information easily accessible. Storing information in your phone is good, but if you lose your phone or can't access the data stored on your phone you would need a Plan B. If you email the information to yourself then you can use someone else's device to get into your email and get the details.

Also email yourself a photo of your passport page and the telephone numbers on the back of your credit cards and debit cards. In the event that you do get pickpocketed or lose your wallet, you'll need to be able to contact your bank and report your cards missing. You don't need to include anything more than the last 4 digits of the card number – the bank has it anyway, but it helps them to identify which card you are calling about.

Entrust a Sensible Person

It's a good idea to have someone sensible at home with a copy of your itinerary and the ability to retrieve your passport information if needed. I say someone sensible because if something does go sideways on your trip, chances are you will already be stressed out and having to deal with hysteria or disinterest from home will just make things worse.

If you are traveling alone choose some method of checking in with this sensible person daily. It can be as simple as a quick WhatsApp message each day. Whether you are a guy or a girl, a man or a woman, as a solo traveler you need someone to know if you slip off the grid, and where you were last known to be. Let's face it, as much as we love the freedom of solo travel anything can happen. If you get in an accident, have a medical calamity or find yourself on the wrong side of trouble, someone needs to know that you are MIA.

Roll with It

The most important piece of advice I can give you about things going wrong, or not exactly as planned, is to just roll with it. Don't let it ruin your trip. It's a nuisance, it's inconvenient, but remember you saved and made sacrifices to be here, so shake it off and move on.

My Glam Italia traveler whose luggage didn't arrive until two days before she flew home could have pouted and cried and been miserable about it. She had planned every detail of every fabulous outfit she had saved up for and bought for her big trip, but she didn't let it spoil her fun. She kept a great attitude, bought some local shoes and clothes, and got on with having a great time.

CHAPTER TWENTY-THREE
What to Do If You Get Sick in Italy

The staff at the Farmacia are rock stars...

We don't ever plan on getting sick while when we travel, but what should you do if it does happen? Coming down with a cold, a tummy bug or an upper respiratory infection can ruin your trip, and you have saved too hard and been planning too long to get here and let it all go to waste.

Here is my advice on utilizing the medical system in Italy.

Come Prepared
First Aid Kit

I always recommend packing a little first aid kit for your trip. You don't want to get home after a long day of sightseeing and have to head back out to find a farmacia to buy band aids for your blisters or aloe for your sunburned neck. It is far easier to pull them from your suitcase.

Your first aid kit should include:

1. Basic Medicines
In addition to band aids and aloe, you should pack small sizes of over-the-counter remedies that work for you. Things such as Excedrine if

you get headaches, Dayquil and Nyquil gelcaps, Immodium or Pepto – the tried and tested remedies that you would take if you were uncomfortable at home. You won't find these same products on the store shelves in Italy, and no matter how great the Italian products are, it is reassuring to have with you the medicines that you already know work for you.

2. Vitamins

I always at least try to take more vitamins in the week prior to leaving for an overseas trip, and take plenty more while I am traveling, in the hope they will help me to ward off any colds. So far it seems to have worked pretty well.

3. Disinfectant Wipes

I am that crazy person who gets on a plane and immediately wipes down every surface I might touch with disinfectant wipes. Airplanes are really germy places. Your seat area is not cleaned between flights, so whatever germs the person sitting there before you had, you are now exposed to. If they were coughing or sneezing or sweating with a fever, you now own those germs.

I used to think people were paranoid when I would see them wiping down all the surfaces around their plane seat or spraying them with Lysol, until I caught an upper respiratory infection on a 14- hour flight to Australia. I woke up on Day 3 of the trip of a lifetime, thinking I had an elephant sitting on my chest and gasping to try and get a breath. The doctor in the beach town we were staying in said he sees it all the time. He said that airplanes are full of germs, and that I should clean my area with disinfectant wipes when I fly. Duly noted! I have never taken a flight since without first cleaning my seat area and tray table.

4. BAKING SODA

I only learned this trick relatively recently but trust me it is worth its weight in gold! I pack about a quarter cup / few tablespoons of baking soda in a zip-lock bag and bring it in my suitcase. Baking soda can be used in many situations to make things better. I haven't yet had a tummy ache while away, but apparently it is good as an antacid. You can mix it with water to make a paste to take out the sting of sunburn. But the big lifesaver is for mosquito bites. I get eaten alive in Italy! (Actually, I get eaten alive anywhere that there are biting bugs.) If we are there at the same time you will be quite safe because every Italian mosquito will bypass you and come straight for me! To make matters worse I don't just get bitten and get itchy. I am the person who gets giant angry welts from mosquito bites that look like red golf balls. (Okay, so that's an exaggeration, but I do get raised, red bumps that look ugly.)

If you get any kind of insect bite, wherever you are in the world, take a little baking soda, mix it with as many drops of water as you need in order to turn the powder into a paste, then paint it on top of the bite, or in my case the bites. Once it has dried just dust it off rather than rinsing it. Baking soda takes out the redness, the swelling and the itch. It is the best remedy ever! I never travel without it now, no matter where I am going.

If You Get Sick While You Are Away

So, if the unplanned happens and you do get sick, what should you do?

In Case of Emergency

Police   113

Ambulance   118

Fire   115

General   112

If it's not an emergency but you just get sick, your first stop is to the pharmacy or Farmacia. These are easy to find because they have a big green cross outside. Normally it is a neon green cross over the door. In America most pharmacies are part of giant chains, but in Italy, like everything else, they are mostly owner-operated. The people working in the Farmacia are very well-trained and can handle most of the common ailments. Be prepared to answer many questions. The pharmacist will ask in-depth questions before handing out medications. They are absolute rock stars at figuring out what is wrong, and which is the best course of treatment. If you go to the Farmacia because you have a bad cough, they will ask you every conceivable question about your cough then recommend a product based on your answers. (If you do have a cough they will ask you if it is a dry cough or a wet cough. They are trying to figure out if you are coughing up nasty stuff or if you have a more rasping, wheezy dry cough.) They tend to get it right as well.

Frequently their first recommendation will be an all-natural product. My readers from Australia and New Zealand will already be familiar with this, my American readers possibly not quite so much. Some of the most effective remedies are non-pharmaceutical. In my experience they'll direct you to a non-pharmaceutical solution first, and if that doesn't work they then give you an over-the-counter pharmaceutical. If, after all their questions, they think you need to see a doctor they will normally have someone they can recommend.

If you are staying in a hotel, the concierge or the front desk will normally be able to call a doctor for you.

If you are staying in a vacation rental apartment, there will usually be a folder with information for you on everything from how to work the washing machine to where to find good restaurants. There should also be information about which doctor to call. If there isn't, ask your landlord to help you. I have stayed in many, many vacation rentals in Italy and have always found the landlords to be incredibly helpful with everything you can possibly think of.

Another option is to call your travel insurance company. The one that I use will find you a doctor nearby who speaks your primary language.

The Doctor's Visit

If you do go to the doctor be prepared to pay in cash. Ask what it will cost when you call to make the appointment.

In all the years I have been traveling to Italy I have been to the doctor only twice. Both times were for the same illness, a cough I picked up in Belize the week before flying to Italy. The first doctor charged me 50 euros in cash, the second didn't charge me anything.

The first doctor opened a drawer and pulled out a box of antibiotics (the standard prescription dose comes pre-measured in Italy), an inhaler, a nasal spray and some cough medicine, which were all included in the 50-euro fee. He also gave me the names and phone numbers of some other doctors in the towns I would be visiting over the next couple of weeks. In case I got stuck, he also gave me his own contact details in case I had to see a doctor who didn't speak English.

The second doctor I saw was a few weeks later. I had gone to a pharmacy to pick up more cough medicine and they told me I needed to see a doctor and set up the appointment for me. He didn't charge me for the visit and gave me antibiotics from his office and a prescription for cough medicine that the pharmacy filled.

It was all very easy.

Comparable Over-the-counter Medicines

You won't find Advil, Motrin, or Excedrine in Italy, but here are some close equivalents to the American over-the-counter remedies.

Asprin is called *Aspirina.*

Ibuprofen products (like Advil) are called *Brufen, Moment,* and the best one for headaches – *Nurofen.*

Acetominophen products (like Tylenol) are called *Paracetamol, Tachipirina* and *Efferalgan.*

Naproxen products (like Aleve) are called *Momendol, Naprosyn* and *Naproxene.*

Antihistamine products are called *Reactine* and *Zyrtec,* as well as *Telfast* (which is close to the American product Allegra). The pharmacist will no doubt recommend a nasal spray as well.

A really helpful app to have on your smartphone is **Find My Medicine**. It will help you to find the Italian equivalent to what you take at home. (You can use it in other countries too.)

If you feel like you are coming down with a bad cold or flu, get to the pharmacy quickly. They will probably give you *Oscillococcinum* (a natural remedy) if you go within the first 24 hours of feeling unwell. The smartest thing you can do is to take a day off, stay in bed with *Oscillococcinum* or whichever over-the-counter remedy you choose, plenty of fluids, and try to sleep it off. You are better to lose one day of your trip than to get really sick and lose several days.

Apart from the one time I actually needed it, I always travel with Dayquil and Nyquil, American over-the-counter products for bad colds. They don't make you better, but they subdue and delay the symptoms for a while so that hopefully you don't feel super sick while you are away.

Helpful Phrases About Your Health

If the person helping you at the pharmacy or the doctor doesn't speak English, either use the translation app on your smartphone, or use these phrases to tell them what is wrong. Don't worry about trying to pronounce the words – just show the person the phrase.

I feel sick. *Mi sento male* or *Mi sto male* (mah-leh)

I am sick. *Mi sono malato.*

My heart. Il mio cuore.

I can't breathe. Non riesco a respirare.

I have a pain here... (point to where it hurts). Mi fa male qui...

I have a bad headache. Ho mal di testa.

I have back ache. Ho mal di schiena.

I have tooth ache. Ho mal di denti.

I am seasick/I get seasick. Ho mal di mare.

I have a cold. Ho il raffreddore.

I have a tummy ache/stomach ache. Ho mal di panica.

I think I have a stomach virus. Penso di avere un virus allo stomaco.

I have allergies. Ho delle allergie.

I have a dry cough. Ho la tosse secca.

I have a chest cough. Ho la tosse grassa.

My throat hurts. Mi fa male la gola.

I have earache. Ho male all'orecchio.

I have a fever. Ho la febbre.

I have sunburn. Mi sono scottato al sole.

I have mosquito bites. Ho punture di zanzare.

If something drastic happens to someone you are traveling with, such as a heart attack or a stroke, or a bad car accident, you should contact your country's embassy. They will be able to help you.

Travel Insurance

I really cannot stress the importance of travel insurance enough. I emphatically recommend buying travel insurance to travelers on my Glam Italia tours, and here is why: anything can happen. That's just life.

If you do wind up in hospital in Italy you will probably be in good hands, and unlike in America it will not break the bank. However, you need to factor in what happens next and how you will get home.

My biggest concern when buying travel insurance is the medical aspect. The policy that I buy covers the cost of getting me back to America with a nurse should anything really drastic happen. Any time you buy insurance you do so in the hope you'll never need to use it, but should that need arise you want to be well-covered.

EVEN MORE SO IF TRAVELLING VIA THE US...

For any of you who will be traveling through America on your way to and from Europe, make sure you have adequate medical travel insurance to cover any time you spend in the US (sometimes you have to stipulate this separately). Again, chances are very slim that anything will go wrong while you are in transit, but American medical costs are insanely high and can easily bankrupt anyone, let alone travelers.

CHAPTER TWENTY-FOUR
Don't Be an "Ugly American"

If it is so much better at home, stay there.

I was going to title this chapter "Etiquette" but thought with that title many readers might be tempted to skip it, and this is important. Regardless of what country you are from, when traveling in Italy (or any other country) don't be the "Ugly American" (AKA the disrespectful tourist).

WHEN IN ROME, DO AS THE ROMANS DO.

When you are in your own country you can act however you choose, but when you are travelling it is important to observe the customs of the country you are in.

COVER UP INSIDE CHURCHES AND CATHEDRALS.

Most churches and cathedrals in Italy require you to have your shoulders covered and be wearing at least a knee length skirt or pants. If you are wearing a sleeveless or bare shouldered top or dress, keep a big scarf in your handbag to throw over your shoulders before entering. If you know there is a likelihood that you will be going to a church, don't wear shorts that day. Or don't go inside the church – your choice.

DON'T BE RUDE.

Bad manners are bad manners. You are a guest in their country, so be polite to the locals. No one (including other tourists) wants to hear that you have a bigger or better one at home. No one cares that you have more electricity, more internet, faster WiFi or a clothes dryer at home. If it is so much better at home, stay there.

APPRECIATE THE DIFFERENCES.

Chances are you will find some of the conveniences that you enjoy at home are not available where you are staying in Italy, or in Italy at all. So, what? We don't travel to have everything identical to home. Remember, you came here to experience Italy, not to compare it to home. Things are probably done differently here than in your home country. Don't compare. Don't complain.

RESPECT THE COFFEE CULTURE.

I once watched an entitled 20-something stamp her foot and shout at a barista that he should be able to make her a venti caramel macchiato like they do at Starbucks. It was cringe worthy! Remember this is *not* the land of the double decaf skinny latte. This is the land of the espresso.

ORDER YOUR MEAL AS IT IS ON THE MENU.

Some restaurants and trattorias may accommodate changes but in general Italian food is served as is. If you are ordering fat-free ranch on the side, hold the onions, hold the cheese, swap out the artichoke for green beans etc, you will drive them insane. Firstly, they are not always able to do this. Secondly, in Italy food is everything. Food is freshly grown on local farms, the flavors of meals are well considered, often from recipes that have been in the family for generations, and they are blended to perfection. Such requests can come across as being very insulting. If you are high maintenance with food and require changes to restaurant menus, think about packing your fat-free ranch in your suitcase (you won't find it on the shelves in supermarkets in Italy). You might be better off to stay in a vacation rental apartment or villa and make your own meals – which, by the way, is fabulous fun anyway!

FOR GOD'S SAKE, DON'T BE HARPING ON ABOUT HOW THE WINE AT HOME IS BETTER.

If nothing else, it makes you look ignorant. If you want Californian wine, or if you truly do believe that Californian wine is better, go to California! I once had the misfortune to be seated next to a couple of wine-whiners on a train. They told me they lived in Sonoma and were wine snobs, so they couldn't really drink the wine in Italy because the wine was so much better in California. It was all I could do not to push them out the window! (Fortunately, the windows on high-speed trains don't open). Italy is renowned for its incredible wine. The wine from your country might be great too but know that you will impress no one by bleating on about how great it is. You will look rude and stupid.

THE INTERNET INFRASTRUCTURE MAY NOT BE AS GOOD AS THE ONE AT HOME.

WiFi may not be as fast or as accessible. Some places may not even have WiFi. If internet access is really important to you, rent or buy an internet hotspot, buy a local phone, or swap out your SIM card. You have options, so use them!

DON'T EXPECT EVERYONE TO SPEAK ENGLISH (OR YOUR PRIMARY LANGUAGE).

In most big tourist areas many people speak English, but not everyone does. In more remote areas, fewer people do. Often they understand English but are uncomfortable trying to speak it. Regardless, remember that you are in their country, so at least make an effort to try to speak their language.

CHAPTER TWENTY-FIVE
Useful Italian Phrases

Buongiorno!

One of the best things you can do when you travel to a foreign country is to learn a few helpful words and phrases in the language of that country.

No one will expect you to be fluent in their language. Even in the more remote parts of Italy most people seem to have at least an understanding of English, so when you begin a conversation or a question in Italian it is more about being polite than anything else.

I do recommend getting a translation app on your smartphone. I use **iTranslate**. If you get stuck, you can at least type in your question in English (or your native language if English is not a comfortable language for you) and it will translate it into Italian. No one will be offended if you show them your translated question instead of trying to speak it.

I speak conversational Italian quite well now, but I don't know medical Italian, or how to speak about cars, or politics or anything particularly important. If I had to explain that I have a flat tire, or I have run out of gas, or if I had to fill out paperwork in Italian (none of which has ever happened to me), I would use my translation app.

I think the most important things to know in any foreign language are the greetings and please and thank you, so let's start there.

Pronouncing Italian

Italian words almost always end in a vowel.

a is pronounced *ah*

e is pronounced *eh*

i is pronounced *ee*

o is pronounced *oh*

Basics

HELLO

There are several ways to say hello. If it is daytime, before around 4pm you will say *Buongiorno. Ciao* also works but is probably used more amongst people who know each other well. *Salve* is another way to say hello. After 4pm-ish you will notice people slip over to *Buona sera* or just *Sera*, which means *Good evening. Buona notte* is for *Goodnight.*

Buongiorno (bwon-JOOR-no). Hello (before 4pm).

Ciao (chow). Hello (before 4pm and amongst friends).

Salve (sal-veh). Hello.

Buona sera (bwona sarah). Good evening (after 4pm).

Sera (sarah). Good evening (abbreviated).

Buona notte (bwona not-eh). Good night.

GOODBYE

For goodbye you can use *arrivederci*, *ciao*, or *a dopo*. Sometimes you will hear *a domani* which means until tomorrow or *a presto,* which means later.

Arrivederci (a-reeve-a-dare-chee). Goodbye.

Ciao (chow). Goodbye.

A dopo (ah-dop-oh). Goodbye.

A domani (ah-doh-mah-nee). Goodbye (until tomorrow).

A presto (ah-press-toe). Later.

MIND YOUR MANNERS

Per favor (pear- fah-vour). Please.

Grazie (grat-zee-eh). Thank you.

Si (see). Yes.

No. No.

Non capisco (non cap-ees-co). I don't understand.

Non lo so (non-low-soh). I don't know.

There are two different types of excuse me. One is to get someone's attention, the other is if you need to move past someone or if you have bumped into someone.

Scusi dov e'…? (skoo-zee, dov-eh…?) Excuse me, where is the…?

Scusi, mi sono perso/persa (for a male it is pers**o** for a female pers**a**) Excuse me, I'm lost…?

Permesso (pear-mess-oh). Excuse me (if you need to move past someone or have bumped into them).

Hot and Cold Food

When you are ordering food knowing how to order hot or cold comes in handy. If you want your sandwich (panino) heated, you would ask for it *caldo*. *Caldo* is hot. *Freddo* is cold.

By the way, one sandwich is **un panino**. If there is more than one sandwich it becomes **panini**. Here in America, an Italian sandwich is often referred to as a panini, which could cause confusion if you were in Italy!

Do you speak English?

Never start a conversation with "Do you speak English?" or assume that someone speaks English (or whichever language you speak). Instead begin with:

Mi dispiace ma non parlo Italiano. Parla inghlese? I'm sorry, but I don't speak Italian. Do you speak English?

Even if you show someone this phrase typed out on your phone instead of trying to say it, it is less rude than just demanding they speak to you in English. If I find a phrase that is too wordy or too difficult for me to say, I normally ask for help to say it correctly. No one ever minds, and they get a kick out of the fact that I'm trying.

Shopping

The most common phrase you will probably use while shopping is to ask how much something costs.

Scusi, quanto costa? Excuse me, how much does this cost?

Scusi, dove sono i camerini? (doh-veh) Excuse me, where are the changing rooms?

C'e' uno sconto? (c'e' is pronounced chay) Is there a discount?

Posso paghare con una carta/una carta di credito? Can I pay with a card/credit card?

Dining Out

The most important thing to know when ordering is that you don't ever say *voglio* which means "I want". Instead you say *vorrei* (vor-ray) which means "I would like". *I want* is demanding and may be considered rude.

Vorrei un bichiere di vino rosso/bianco locale per favor. I would like a local red/white wine please.

Directions

A sinistra (ah-sin-EE-strah) Left.

A destra (ah-DEST-rah) Right.

Dritto (DRITT-oh) Straight.

Come? (CO-meh) How?

Dov'e'? (DOH-veh) Where is?

Quando? (KWAN-doh) When?

Ingresso (in-GRESS-oh) Entrance.

Uscita (ooh-SHEET-ah) Exit.

Aiuto! (eye-YOU-toh) Help!

CHAPTER TWENTY-SIX
Postcards from Italy

One last favorite trick.

Years ago, I started this really lovely travel routine, and now have most of my Glam Italia groups doing it also.

Prepaid Postcards

On the day we arrive in Italy we stop at the Tabacchi and buy stamps. Tabacchi stores are easy to find with their large T signs outside. You can buy tobacco products there (Europeans still smoke – a lot), but also this is where you buy bus tickets (*biglietti*), candy, gum, pens and pencils, bottles of water, and postage stamps (*francobolli*). We each buy enough stamps to send home one postcard per day. Some people buy more so they can send to family and friends as well.

With stamps already purchased, every day we buy a postcard wherever we are, and at the end of the day send ourselves a note about something fun or quirky that happened that day. Maybe it is a note about a fabulous dessert we tried and the name of the restaurant we ate at, or the funny story a waiter told us. Perhaps it's the story of the gorgeous Swedish woman we met in Florence, who works in the little shoe shop and whose Italian husband makes beautiful shoes by hand, as his family has done for centuries.

These postcards are not about saying "*Today I went to the Colosseum*", although going to the Colosseum *is* wonderful and might be perfect for a postcard to the family. You will always remember that you went to the Colosseum, but the random little experiences that flesh out the magic of your trip tend to slip away after a while. That's why I write them down and mail them to myself.

Some of the postcards will probably arrive before you get home, others will arrive each day or across a few weeks. I have had postcards take as long as three weeks to arrive. As each postcard arrives in your mailbox you get to relive a little moment that was special to you.

As you move on in life, these postcards become little treasures that tell an important part of your story. I still have postcards I mailed myself from Egypt 30 years ago. When I look at them they bring back a flood of memories. I also have photos that remind me of the places I went while I was there, but the postcards give me bite-sized pieces of the little stories I had forgotten over time.

Journal

I also recommend writing a journal while you are away. I keep a glue stick in my bag and glue the entry tickets from places we have visited, business cards, and any photos I might print out along the way. I journal about where we went, who we met, where and what we ate. I include as many details as I can remember. I use these journals not only to relive the places I have traveled to, but also as a reference for future trips. Friends always ask me about restaurants, tour guides, places off the beaten track to visit and things to do. I have stacks of journals with everything recorded. I write only on the right page and leave the left page blank to glue photos onto when I get home.

Trust me, if you send yourself postcards and journal your trip, you will treasure those mementos forever.

FINAL THOUGHTS

Thank you for reading my book!

My goal when writing this book was to help you plan a trip that is extra special and tailored to *you* and the things *you* want to see and do.

I hope you will venture off the beaten path, explore different regions of Italy, try different foods and wines, and chase down all the wonderful experiences that are waiting there for you.

In the big, famous cities, I hope you will see the big tourist attractions, but also wander the smaller streets, and discover the personality of the city that sometimes gets hidden behind all the tourism.

I hope you will take me with you to Italy as an e-book on your phone and find me easy to scroll through when you need quick references to food and wines, help at the pharmacy, or assistance in a train station!

Lastly, I know you want to race around and see as many things as possible while you are in this beautiful country. Make sure you slow down, take time to savor everything around you, talk to the locals, and enjoy a prosecco in a little piazza at the end of the afternoon as the sun goes down...

RESOURCES

Keep in touch

Thank you so much for reading my book! I hope you enjoyed it and found some great information for your travels. If you found this book helpful, if it has saved you some money on flights or accommodation, or if you have just enjoyed reading it, please take two minutes to write me a review on Amazon. Your review matters, and I thank you in advance for writing it!

Let's stay connected

My goal with this book was to help you plan your dream trip, show you some different options, maybe introduce you to some new ways of traveling, help you out while you are in Italy, and more than anything to help you to make this the absolute trip of a lifetime. But it doesn't end there.

WEBSITE

Check out my website at www.CorinnaCooke.com

FREE RESOURCES

Throughout this book I have talked about my Free Resources. This is a set of PDF's that you can print out and use to plan your perfect trip. I give these PDF's to all my Glam Italia Tour travelers when we are planning their tour and also the checklists included in this bundle to help make sure everything is taken care of in the right timeframe, from ordering passports to checking in with your cell-phone company to making sure everything at home is ready for you to leave. You can download them then print off as many times as you need from **www.glamitaliabooks.com/freeresources**

MONTHLY NEWSLETTER

My bi-weekly newsletter focuses on lovely, off the beaten track towns to visit, foods, festivals and fascinating things to do in Italy. It's all about helping you to frame out a more interesting trip. You only hear from me twice each month but you'll want to keep these newsletters in their own email folder for reference down the line. In all likelihood you will end up coming back to Italy again, so items that don't quite fit this upcoming trip may work for you somewhere in the future. (On your next trip!)

You can join the newsletter on my website, **www.CorinnaCooke.com**

MORE BOOKS

I have more books in the *Glam Italia – How to Travel Italy* series. You can find my books on my website, www.CorinnaCook.com or on my Amazon page, Corinna Cooke

CORINNA B'S WORLD BLOG

I have been blogging about Italy for years on my Corinna B's World blog. There is a wealth of information on there about places to go and things to do in Italy. You can find all of it in the Travel section.

PINTEREST @CORINNAMAKEUP

I would love to see you on Pinterest too! I have Pinterest boards for many cities and regions in Italy, all tying back to either my blog or someone else's. You can quickly find information about places you are going or places you may be interested in visiting. My Pinterest is @CorinnaMakeup

INSTAGRAM

And finally, I would love to see you on Instagram! Follow my personal account @CorinnaTravels. Please tag me in your Italy photos and use the hashtag #HowToTravelItaly so that I can watch your trip.

If you have the paperback copy of this book, please post a photo of it somewhere fun in Italy and don't forget to tag me!

Arrivederci!

ABOUT THE AUTHOR

Corinna Cooke is an international Makeup Artist, Blogger and Magazine Beauty Editor. Her non-stop travels to Italy and subsequent blog posts resulted in an "accidental" boutique, private tour guiding business. For two months every year she takes small groups of women on glamour-filled, a la carte tours of Italy, where feeling fabulous happens at affordable, real person prices.

Corinna lives in Phoenix with her son, two cats and rescue dog called Frankie.

Visit her at CorinnaBsWorld.com

Made in United States
North Haven, CT
03 April 2023

34955323R00146